SPARKNOTES™
101
Spanish

SPARK PUBLISHING

Author: Rebecca J. Ortman

Reviewers: Judith E. Liskin-Gasparro, Ph.D., and
           Kathleen Angelique Dwyer

Spark Publishing
120 Fifth Avenue
New York, NY 10011
www.sparknotes.com

ISBN-10: 1-4114-0438-6
ISBN-13: 978-1-4114-0438-0

Please submit all changes or report errors to www.sparknotes.com/errors

Printed and bound in the United States.

Library of Congress Cataloging-in-Publication Data

SparkNotes 101 Spanish.
        p. cm.
    Includes bibliographical references and index.
    ISBN-13: 978-1-4114-0438-0 (alk. paper)
    1. Spanish language—Textbooks for foreign speakers—English.
    I. Title: SparkNotes one hundred one Spanish. II. Title: SparkNotes one hundred and one Spanish. III. SparkNotes LLC.

PC4129.E5S685 2006
468.2'421—dc22
                                                2005024628

Contents

A Note from SparkNotes

Welcome to the *SparkNotes 101* series! This book will help you succeed in your introductory college Spanish course.

Every component of this study guide has been designed to help you process the course material more quickly and score higher on your exams. You'll see lots of headings, lists, charts, and, most important, no long blocks of text. This format will allow you to quickly situate yourself and easily get to the crux of your course. We've organized the book in the following manner:

Lessons 1–11: Each lesson provides a clarification of material included in your textbook. Key features include:

- **Functional Language:** This section moves beyond sentence structure and grammar points to present you with chunks of language that you can use in everyday conversation in class to sound like a native speaker. You will find one "Functional Language" section at the end of each lesson.

- **Sample Test Questions:** These show you the kinds of questions you are most likely to encounter on a test. There is one set at the end of every lesson, and answer keys to every exercise are included at the back of the book.

- **Text Boxes:** Throughout, text boxes call out main points and provides related information. Watch for the **Pitfall!** boxes, which point out particular grammar issues and irregularities that might trip you up. They'll give you the secrets that the language experts know.

Appendices: The appendices provide a list of commonly used vocabulary words; verb charts for all the verbs used in the book; a description of accent marks, including a section on rules and use; and answers to all of the sample test questions.

Index: Use the index at the back of the book to make navigation easier or to look up specific topics.

We hope *SparkNotes 101: Spanish* helps you, gives you confidence, and occasionally saves your butt! Your input makes us better. Let us know what you think or how we can improve this book at www.sparknotes.com.

Introduction

More than 400 million people worldwide speak Spanish today. It's the predominant language in twenty countries, and many people across the globe have learned Spanish as a second language. In fact, it's the third most commonly spoken language after English and Chinese. According to the most recent U.S. Census, people of Hispanic origin constitute the largest racial or ethnic minority in the United States, about 14 percent of the total population. The number of Hispanics is expected to continue rising in the country, making Spanish a very useful language to learn.

THE HISTORY OF SPANISH

Spanish originated sometime before the sixth century B.C. on the Iberian Peninsula (present-day Spain and Portugal) with the region's first inhabitants, the Iberians, who mingled with a nomadic people from central Europe, the Celts. The two groups evolved into the Celtiberians and spoke a form of Celtic. Several centuries later, in 19 B.C., the area fell under Roman rule and became known as Hispania. When Latin, the language of the Romans, mixed with the languages of the Celtiberians, a new language called "Vulgar Latin" appeared.

In the 1200s, King Alfonso X began to standardize Spanish across the peninsula and chose Castilian, a Vulgar Latin dialect, as the language of all governmental documents. In 1492, monarchs Isabella of Castile and Ferdinand of Aragón made Castilian the official dialect of their entire kingdom. The Castilian dialect became the educational and written standard in Spain and is the language that we know as Spanish today.

REGIONAL VARIATIONS

Modern Spanish varies from region to region. The Spanish spoken in Madrid is slightly different from that spoken in Mexico City, Lima, or New York, just like the English in London differs somewhat from that spoken in Sydney or Chicago. Accents are the most noticeable difference, but some vocabulary words and expressions vary as well. For example, in England you would use the word *bin*, while in the United States the same object would be called a "trash can." Similarly, in Puerto Rico you would use the word *guagua* but in Ecuador you would use *autobus*; both mean "bus." The majority of the structures and vocabulary are identical from Spanish-speaking country to country, however, so the differences might result only in slight misunderstandings. A good grasp of the basics will allow conversation with Spanish speakers across the world.

SPANGLISH

Many Spanish speakers, primarily in the United States, have adopted a manner of speaking that mixes English and Spanish. Colloquially called "Spanglish," this hybrid is common in areas of close border contacts, such as Southern California and Mexico, and in areas with large Hispanic populations, such as New York City and Miami. As with pure Spanish, Spanglish varies from region to region. New York City Spanglish is different from Los Angeles Spanglish, and both differ from Miami Spanglish.

Several types of this emerging dialect exist. In the most common sort, called "code switching," a person speaks in a mixture of Spanish and English. For example, "*Vamos* to the library" (Let's go to the library), or "*No estoy listo* because I have to shower" (I'm not ready because I have to shower). Sometimes English words are pronounced and spelled in a Spanish style and used in place of Spanish words. For example, Spanglish speakers might say *lonche* rather than *almuerzo* (lunch), and *vacumear* instead of *pasar la aspiradora* (to vacuum). Another type of Spanglish occurs when speakers use English syntax when speaking Spanish, for example, putting the adjective before the noun, rather than after it.

This intermingling of words and cultures, with many variations and speakers, shows no signs of abating. With the expected rise in numbers of Hispanics in the United States, it's exciting to think about how the Spanish language will grow and transform in the future.

Lesson 1

The Spanish Alphabet

Pronunciation

- Vowel Sounds
- Consonant Sounds
- Double Consonants
- Stress
- Diphthongs

Cognates

- Patterns
- Cognate Adjectives
- False Friends
- Crossover Words

Functional Language: Greetings, Leave-taking, and Introductions

Sample Test Questions

1

You may have one or two years of high school Spanish under your belt, or you may be brand new to the language. Either way, it's a good idea to familiarize yourself with the absolute basics of Spanish before you dive into more complex sentence structures.

The Spanish Alphabet

First things first. Here are the letters of the Spanish alphabet and their Spanish pronunciation. As you read them, say them out loud.

a	(ah)	k	(kah)	s	(ES-seh)
b	(beh)	l	(EL-eh)	t	(teh)
c	(seh)	m	(EH-meh)	u	(oo)
d	(deh)	n	(EH-neh)	v	(veh)
e	(eh)	ñ	(EH-nyeh)	w	(DOH-bleh veh)
f	(EH-feh)	o	(oh)	x	(EH-kees)
g	(heh)	p	(peh)	y	(ee-gree-EH-ga)
h	(AH-cheh)	q	(koo)	z	(SEH-tah)
i	(ee)	r	(EH-reh)		
j	(HO-tah)	rr	(EH-reh) with trill		

You won't see any surprises here, other than the double *r* and the *ñ*. And even these two letters are most likely familiar to you, due to the constant interaction these days between Spanish and English.

If you've studied Spanish before, you probably already know about the letters *ch* and *ll*: they used to be considered separate letters. In today's Spanish alphabet and dictionary entries, this is no longer the case. *Ch*, instead of coming between *c* and *d*, now comes between *ce* and *ci*.

La Real Academia Española La Real Academia Española is the institution responsible for regulating the Spanish language. In 1994, it agreed to remove ch and ll from the alphabet by request of UNESCO and other international organizations. The change was made to simplify dictionaries, to make Spanish more compatible with English, and to aid in translations.

Pronunciation

Spanish is a phonetic language. In other words, you can easily guess the pronunciation of a word from its written form. Letters are always pronounced the same way, except for slight variations that are due to accent marks. In this section, we will look at the pronunciation of vowels and consonants in Spanish.

VOWEL SOUNDS

Vowels are hard to master in any language. Consider this: in English, *rough*, *dough*, *cough*, and *through* all have the same combination of letters but are pronounced differently. However, you are in luck. Spanish, unlike English, is a phonetic language, meaning that words usually sound the way they look. The three different pronunciations of the same groups of letters in the example above would never happen in a phonetic language. Even so, Spanish vowels are challenging to the English-speaker.

Try practicing the following Spanish vowels aloud.

▶ **a**
pronounced *ah*, as in the English word "yacht"

casa (CAH-sah) *house*
gato (GAH-toh) *cat*
falda (FAHL-dah) *skirt*

▶ **e**
pronounced *eh*, as in the English word *ten*

pez (pehs) *fish*
mesa (MEH-sah) *table*
ver (vehr) *to see*

▶ **i**
pronounced *ee*, as in the English word "see"

libro (LEE-broh) *book*
silla (SEE-yah) *chair*
comida (coh-MEE-dah) *food*

5

LESSON 1

▶ **o**
pronounced *oh*, as in the English word "rose"

> **flor** (flohr) *flower*
> **vaso** (VAH-soh) *cup*
> **oro** (OH-roh) *gold*

▶ **u**
pronounced *oo*, as in the English word "moon"

> **duro** (DOO-roh) *hard*
> **atún** (ah-TOON) *tunafish*
> **punta** (POON-tah) *point*

CONSONANT SOUNDS

Most Spanish consonants, luckily, are pronounced just like in English. Here are the ones that are not.

▶ **b** and **v**
pronounced roughly the same, like an English *b*

> **banda** (BAHN-dah) *band*
> **vela** (BEH-lah) *sail*

▶ **c**
before *a*, *o*, and *u*, pronounced like an English *k*

> **casa** (CAH-sah) *house*
> **cosa** (COH-sah) *thing*
> **cuna** (COO-nah) *crib*

▶ **c**
before *e* and *i*, pronounced like the English *ss*

> **ceja** (SEH-hah) *eyebrow*
> **cita** (SEE-tah) *appointment*

▶ **g**
before *a*, *o*, and *u*, pronounced like an English *g*

> **gracias** (GRAH-seeahs) *thank you*
> **gota** (GOH-tah) *drop*
> **gusto** (GOOS-toh) *taste*

▶ **g**
before *e* and *i*, pronounced like an English *h*

> **gente** (HEHN-teh) *people*
> **gitano** (hee-TAH-noh) *gypsy*

▶ **g**
before *ui* and *ue*, pronounced like an English *g*

> **guía** (GHEE-ah) *guide*
> **guerra** (GHE-rrah) *war*

▶ **h**
silent!

> **hacha** (AH-chah) *axe*
> **almohada** (ahl-moh-AH-dah) *pillow*

▶ **j**
pronounced like an English *h*

> **jardín** (har-DEEN) *garden*
> **ajo** (AH-hoh) *garlic*

▶ **ñ**
pronounced like the *ny* in *canyon*

> **año** (AH-nyoh) *year*
> **piña** (PEE-nyah) *pineapple*

▶ **q**
before *ue* or *ui*, pronounced like an English *k*

> **queso** (KEH-soh) *cheese*
> **aquí** (ah-KEE) *here*

▶ **z**
pronounced like an English *s*

zapato (sah-PAH-toh) *shoe*

> **The Spanish Z** *In many parts of Spain, z is pronounced like an English th. Zapato, therefore, is pronounced tha-PAH-toh.*

DOUBLE CONSONANTS

As we have seen, Spanish still has two double consonants that are often considered single letters: *ll* and *rr*.

▶ **ll**
pronounced like an English *y*

llave (YAH-veh) *key*
olla (OH-yah) *pot*

▶ **rr**
pronounced like a heavily rolled *r*

arroz (ah-RROHS) *rice*
horror (oh-RROR) *horror*

> **Ll and Rr** *Try to remember to pronounce ll and rr correctly, or you may confuse Spanish speakers. For example, the word caro (expensive) is pronounced differently than the word carro (car).*

STRESS

Stressing Spanish words is generally straightforward. If an accent mark (´) isn't present, the stress is generally on the last or second-to-last syllable of the word. Here are some rules.

▶ If a word ends in a consonant other than *n* or *s*, stress the last syllable.

papel (pah-PEL) *paper*
actriz (ahk-TREESS) *actress*

▶ If the last syllable ends in *n*, *s*, or a vowel, the second-to-last syllable is stressed.

> casa   (CAH-sah)   *house*
> martes   (MAHR-tehs)   *Tuesday*

▶ If an accent mark is present, the accented vowel receives the stress.

> camión   (cah-MEE<u>OHN</u>)   *truck*
> sábado   (SAH-bah-<u>doh</u>)   *Saturday*

DIPHTHONGS

Diptongos, or diphthongs, are vowel combinations. Diphthongs are made up of a weak vowel and strong vowel, or two weak vowels, that both belong in the same syllable. *I* and *u* are considered weak vowels, while *a*, *e*, and *o* are considered strong vowels.

Diphthongs are pronounced as a single syllable. However, the stress within the syllable varies slightly, depending on the particular vowel combination.

When the diphthong is made up of a weak and a strong vowel, stress the strong vowel.

> **cua**ndo (pronounced KOO<u>OAHN</u>-doh)   *when*
>
> weak   strong

When the diphthong is made up of two weak vowels, stress the second one.

> **Sui**za (pronounced SOO<u>EE</u>-sah)   *Switzerland*
>
> weak   weak

Note: Since a diphthong is a combination of vowels that belong in the same syllable, two strong vowels side by side *do not* make up a diphthong.

When you do see two strong vowels, though, separate them into two syllables.

feo (pronounced FEH-oh) *ugly*

strong   strong

> ***Forget English!*** *In English, when vowels are combined they may develop into a totally new sound. This is not the case in Spanish. For example, you might be inclined to pronounce the Spanish word* Europa *as (yur-OH-pah), based on the English pronunciation. The correct pronunciation of the word is (ehoo-ROH-pah). Each vowel has its own sound, and each sound must be pronounced clearly.*

Cognates
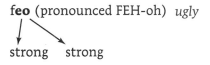

Many Spanish words resemble words in other languages and have identical or similar meanings. These words are called **cognates**. Because of their roots in Latin, the Romance languages have many similarities: if you've studied French, Italian, or Portuguese (or have visited countries where these languages are spoken), you will already have a sizable vocabulary base for Spanish.

Although English is a Germanic language and not a descendant of Latin, it did receive considerable influence from Latin, so many Spanish words should be recognizable to you. There are only minor differences in spelling between English and Spanish cognates.

Take a look at the following words. What do you think they mean?

estación   increíble   paciencia

Hopefully you've guessed that their English equivalents are "station," "incredible," and "patience."

PATTERNS

Cognates are easy to identify because they closely resemble English words. Another way to identify cognates is to look for patterns.

Once you learn the following patterns you'll be able to easily recognize new words.

▶ *-ción* ⟶ -tion

   inmigración   *immigration*
   sensación   *sensation*

▶ *-dad* ⟶ -ty

   curiosidad   *curiosity*
   identidad   *identity*

▶ *-oso/a* ⟶ -ous

   famoso   *famous*
   religiosa   *religious*

▶ *-cia* ⟶ -ce or -cy

   agencia   *agency*
   esencia   *essence*

Many of the names of school subjects in Spanish and English come from the same Latin or Greek roots.

▶ *-ica* ⟶ -ics

   matemática   *mathematics*
   física   *physics*

▶ *-ía* ⟶ -y

   biología   *biology*
   filosofía   *philosophy*

COGNATE ADJECTIVES

Take a look at these words. They are all cognate adjectives that can be used to describe either a male or a female. They do not change form in the singular.

excelente
difícil
egoísta
feminista
idealista
indiferente
intelectual
inteligente
interesante
materialista
natural
horrible
popular
responsable
sentimental

Now take a look at these words. They are cognate adjectives that change form in the singular. Use -o to describe a male, and -a to describe a female.

agresivo/a
famoso/a
generoso/a
impulsivo/a
nervioso/a
honesto/a
romántico/a
sincero/a
tímido/a

FALSE FRIENDS

If a word looks like an English word, it probably means the same thing. However, some words are wolves in sheeps' clothing. Words that look similar but have different meanings are called "false friends."

What do you think the word *librería* means? Library? Wrong! It actually means "bookstore." *Biblioteca* means "library." Here's another false friend that students often find problematic: *embarazada*. It actually means "pregnant." If you want to say that you're embarrassed, use the adjective *avergonzado/a*.

Try to learn the following list of false friends:

> *carpeta:* "folder," NOT "carpet"
> *campo:* "field" or "countryside," NOT "camping"
> *compromiso:* "engagement" or "obligation," NOT "compromise"
> *contestar:* "to answer," NOT "to contest"
> *éxito:* "success," NOT "exit"
> *fábrica:* "factory," NOT "fabric"
> *recordar:* "to remember," NOT "to record"
> *ropa:* "clothes," NOT "rope"
> *sopa:* "soup," NOT "soap"
> *tuna:* "cactus fruit," NOT "tuna fish"

If you are ever unsure as to whether or not a word is a cognate, the best thing to do is look it up in the dictionary.

CROSSOVER WORDS

What's a crossover word? It's one kind of Spanglish, which we discussed in the introduction. You've probably heard about Hispanic singers "crossing over" to the English world. Singers like Ricky Martin, Enrique Iglesias, and Gloria Estefan all started their careers by singing in Spanish. At some point these bilingual stars decided to expand their fan base by singing in English too. Well, crossover words, as you can imagine, are English words that have entered the Spanish language and vice-versa.

There are many examples of Spanish words being absorbed into the English language. Consider the following words:

> fiesta
> mañana
> señorita
> siesta
> tango

There are also examples of English words being absorbed into Spanish. Look at these words.

póster
suéter
sándwich

See, you *do* know some Spanish! Crossover influence makes each language richer. Ricky Martin and Enrique Iglesias crossed over for a reason: they wanted to reach more people. And they were certainly successful.

> **Hispanics in America** *U.S. Census Bureau figures show that in 2002 there were 37.4 million Hispanics living in the United States (13.3 percent of the total population). Considering these figures, it isn't surprising how many crossover words we find in the English and Spanish languages. Clearly, both languages have benefited from the geographic proximity of Mexico and the constant influx of Hispanics into the United States.*
>
> *[U.S. Census Bureau: The Hispanic Population in the United States: March 2002, http://www.census.gov/population/www/socdemo/hispanic/ho02.html]*

Functional Language: Greetings, Leave-taking, and Introductions

In this first "Functional Language" section we'll look at the all-important skills of saying hello and good-bye.

Note: We will cover formal vs. informal forms in Lesson 3.

Use these words and expressions to:

▶ Greet people

Hola.   *Hi.*
Buenos días.   *Good morning.*

Buenas tardes. *Good afternoon.*
Buenas noches. *Good evening/Good night.*
¿Cómo está? *How are you?* (formal)
¿Cómo estás? *How are you?* (informal)

▶ Say goodbye to someone

Hasta luego. *Goodbye/So long.*
Chau. *Bye.*
Nos vemos. *See you.*
Hasta pronto. *Goodbye/Until we meet again.*
Hasta mañana. *See you tomorrow.*

▶ Introduce yourself

Me llamo Rebeca. *My name is Rebeca.* (Literally: I call myself
    Rebeca.)
Yo soy Martín. *I'm Martín.*

▶ Ask someone their name

¿Cómo se llama? *What is your name?* (formal)
¿Cómo te llamas? *What is your name?* (informal)

▶ Excuse yourself

Con permiso. *Excuse me.* (For example, when you're trying
    to get past someone on the subway.)
Perdón. *Excuse me.* (For example, when you've stepped on
    someone's foot, or if you want to get someone's attention
    politely.)

Titles of Respect In Spanish, it's appropriate to use the basic titles
of courtesy—señor (Mr.), señora (Mrs.), and señorita (Miss and
Ms.)—followed by the person's last name. It is also important to
address qualified individuals by any titles they may have, such as
profesor (professor) or licenciado (lawyer). You may also hear
people use the old courtesy titles don and doña (preceding the first
name) to show respect to an older man or woman.

Sample Test Questions

PART 1, Exercise A

The following Spanish words have underlined sounds. Try matching them to their English equivalents. Write the letter in the space provided.

1. *ll*ama _____	a. m<u>oo</u>n
2. ni<u>ñ</u>o _____	b. <u>c</u>at
3. <u>c</u>ine _____	c. ca<u>ny</u>on
4. án<u>g</u>el _____	d. sl<u>ee</u>p
5. <u>u</u>va _____	e. d<u>oo</u>r
6. <u>i</u>nca _____	f. <u>g</u>et
7. <u>c</u>ama _____	g. <u>s</u>it
8. am<u>or</u> _____	h. <u>y</u>es
9. fl<u>e</u>cha _____	i. <u>h</u>elp
10. <u>g</u>orra _____	j. m<u>e</u>t

Exercise B

Look back over the rules of stress in Spanish. Now select which syllable has the correct stress, based on what you've learned. Write the letter in the space provided.

1. *pájaro* _____

    A. pá JA ro
    B. PÁ ja ro
    C. pá ja RO

2. *juvenil* _____

> A. JU ve nil
> B. ju ve NIL
> C. ju VE nil

3. *naranja* _____

> A. NA ran ja
> B. na ran JA
> C. na RAN ja

4. *canciones* _____

> A. can CION es
> B. CAN cion es
> C. can cion ES

5. *corazón* _____

> A. co RA zón
> B. CO ra zón
> C. co ra ZÓN

PART 2, Exercise A

Can you figure out the Spanish equivalents of the following words? Write your answer in the space provided.

1. *sensation* _____

2. *depression* _____

3. *pessimism* _____

4. *invention* _____

5. *celebration* _____

6. *curious* _____

7. *urgent* _____

8. prosperity _____

9. experience _____

10. optimism _____

Exercise B

Identify the following cognates by giving their English equivalents. Write your answer in the space provided.

1. geografía _____

2. artista _____

3. farmacia _____

4. nación _____

5. fabuloso _____

6. paraíso _____

7. humanidad _____

8. dormitorio _____

9. profesor _____

10. museo _____

PART 3, Exercise A

Read the following situations. What do you say? Fill in the blanks with the most appropriate word or phrase. Use each word or phrase once.

Me llamo   Hola   Cómo te llamas
Buenos días   Hasta luego

1. *On your way to dinner, you run into your friend. You say "¡_____, Manuel!"*

2. *You are leaving class. You say "_____" to your professor.*

3. *You meet your roommate's boyfriend for the first time. To introduce yourself, you say "_____ . . ."*

4. *You'd like to know your new lab partner's name. You ask "¿ _____ ?"*

5. *You walk into the bakery, early in the morning. You say "_____ , señora."*

LESSON 1

Lesson 2

Nouns
- Gender
- Number

Numbers
- Numbers 1–30
- *Hay*
- Numbers 31–100

Definite Articles

Indefinite Articles

Present Tense of *Ser*

Functional Language: Telling Time
- Expressions of Time

Sample Test Questions

2

Nouns

Nouns, or *sustantivos*, identify people, places, things, animals, or ideas. Each Spanish nouns has a gender (masculine or feminine) and a number (singular or plural). Let's discuss gender first.

GENDER

In English, nouns do not have a gender. Unfortunately, there is no real rule for determining the gender of a Spanish noun: the gender of each noun must be learned separately. However, there are certain indicators, or hints, that will help you as you work toward fluency in the language.

Word Ending: Masculine

The easiest way to determine the gender of a Spanish noun is to look at its ending. Before you memorize the rules, remember this: as in any language, there are exceptions. In fact, at times there are so many exceptions that you have to wonder why a rule was created at all.

▶ Most nouns that end in *-o* are masculine.

el númer**o**   *the number*
el libr**o**   *the book*

> **EXCEPTIONS** The following nouns are all feminine, even though they end in o
>
> la man**o**   *the hand*
> la radi**o**   *the radio*
> la mot**o**   *the motorcycle*
> la fot**o**   *the photograph*

▶ Most nouns that end in *-l* or *-r* are masculine.

el barri**l**   *the barrel*
el sabo**r**   *the flavor*

EXCEPTIONS *The following nouns are all feminine, even though they end in -l.*

la capital   *the capital city*
la miel   *the honey*
la piel   *the skin*
la sal   *the salt*

▶ Most nouns that end in *–aje* are masculine.

el gar**aje**   *the garage*
el person**aje**   *the character*

Moto and Foto *You might wonder, "Why aren't moto and foto considered masculine nouns? They end in -o, right?"*

There are numerous irregular nouns in Spanish. Most of them must simply be memorized: there is no clear reasoning behind their irregularity. Moto and foto, however, are actually regular. They are both abbreviations for longer words that end in -a: motocicleta and fotografía.

Word Ending: Feminine

▶ Most nouns that end in -a are feminine.

la tiz**a**   *the chalk*
la mes**a**   *the table*

EXCEPTIONS *The following nouns are all masculine, even though they end in -a.*

el d**í**a   *the day*
el poem**a**   *the poem*
el planet**a**   *the planet*
el idiom**a**   *the language*
el pap**á**   *the dad*
el map**a**   *the map*

▶ Most nouns that end in -ad, -ción, -sión, -umbre, and -ud are feminine. Notice, too, that some of these words are cognates of English.

la libert**ad**   *the liberty*
la condi**ción**   *the condition*
la deci**sión**   *the decision*
la cost**umbre**   *the custom*
la sal**ud**   *the health*

Word Ending: Both Feminine and Masculine

▶ Some nouns in Spanish can be feminine or masculine. Look for the -ista ending.

el / la art**ista**   *the artist*
el / la tur**ista**   *the tourist*
el / la pian**ista**   *the pianist*

Meaning: Feminine and Masculine

Another way of determining whether a noun is masculine or feminine is to think about what the word means.

▶ If a noun refers to a male, it is usually masculine.

el rey   *the king*
el toro   *the bull*

▶ If a noun refers to a female, it is usually feminine.

la actriz   *the actress*
la vaca   *the cow*

Names

Most names and titles that end in -o change to -a to form the feminine.

el tí**o** / la tí**a**   *the uncle / the aunt*
el hij**o** / la hij**a**   *the son / the daughter*
el amig**o** / la amig**a**   *the friend* (male) / *the friend* (female)

NUMBER

And now, on to number. In Spanish, it is quite easy to form the plural of a singular noun.

▶ If a noun ends in a vowel, form the plural by adding -s.

el gat**o**   ⟶   los gato**s**   *the cat / the cats*
la plum**a**   ⟶   las pluma**s**   *the pen / the pens*

▶ If a noun ends in a consonant, form the plural by adding **-es**. For nouns that end in -z, change the -z to a -c first.

el relo**j**   ⟶   los reloj**es**   *the watch / the watches*
la actri**z**   ⟶   las actric**es**   *the actress / the actresses*

▶ The plural of nouns that end in -es does not change.

el miércol**es**   ⟶   los miércol**es**   *Wednesday / Wednesdays*

When you are referring to a group that includes both masculine and feminine nouns, use the masculine plural ending.

4 profesoras ⎤
          ⎬ 5 profesores
1 profesor ⎦

Numbers

Before we learn about articles, let's discuss the numbers 1–100 in Spanish. These will come in handy this unit and the next.

NUMBERS 1-30

0	cero	11	once	22	veintidós
1	uno	12	doce	23	veintitrés
2	dos	13	trece	24	veinticuatro
3	tres	14	catorce	25	veinticinco
4	cuatro	15	quince	26	veintiséis
5	cinco	16	dieciséis	27	veintisiete
6	seis	17	diecisiete	28	veintiocho
7	siete	18	dieciocho	29	veintinueve
8	ocho	19	diecinueve	30	treinta
9	nueve	20	veinte		
10	diez	21	veintiuno		

The Number One

In Spanish, the word for "one" has several forms.

▶ When counting, use *uno*.

   uno, dos, tres, etc.

▶ Use *un* before singular, masculine nouns.

   un hombre   *one man*
   un gato   *one cat*

▶ Use *una* before singular, feminine nouns.

   una manzana   *one apple*
   una casa   *one house*

▶ The number *veintiuno* becomes *veintiún* before masculine nouns.

   21 gatos = **veintiún** gatos

▶ The number *veintiuno* becomes *veintiuna* before feminine nouns.

21 manzanas = **veintiuna** manzanas

HAY

▶ Use the word *hay* to say "there is" and "there are" in Spanish. *¿Hay?* asks "is there?" or "are there?"

> **PITFALL!**   *Hay is not the same as "it is." If you want to say "it is," say es.*

Hay un estudiante en la clase.   *There is one student in the classroom.*
¿**Hay** un estudiante en la clase?   *Is there a student in the classroom?*

Hay cinco estudiantes en la clase.   *There are five students in the classroom.*
¿**Hay** cinco estudiantes en la clase?   *Are there five students in the classroom?*

▶ Use *no hay* to say "there is not" and "there are not."

No hay un estudiante en la clase.   *There is not a student in the classroom / There aren't any students in the classroom.*
Noy hay tres estudiantes en la clase.   *There aren't three students in the classroom.*

LESSON 2

LESSON 2

NUMBERS 31–100

31	treinta y uno	50	cincuenta
32	treinta y dos	60	sesenta
33	treinta y tres	70	setenta
34	treinta y cuatro	80	ochenta
35	treinta y cinco	90	noventa
36	treinta y seis	100	cien, ciento
37	treinta y siete		
38	treinta y ocho		
39	treinta y nueve		
40	cuarenta		

Note: beginning with 31, Spanish numbers are written as three separate words. Also, when *uno* is part of a compound number, it becomes *un* before a masculine noun and *una* before a feminine noun.

sesenta y **un** perros   *sixty-one dogs*
treinta y **una** sillas   *thirty-one chairs*

Definite Articles

You've probably noticed that most of the nouns shown as examples have been accompanied by the words *el*, *la*, *los*, or *las*. These are definite articles. Their English equivalent is "the." Definite articles point out something specific. For example, in "the house," "the" points out a specific house.

Try to learn nouns with their articles. This will help you remember whether they are masculine or feminine.

As you can probably guess, feminine nouns are accompanied by the feminine definite article. Masculine nouns are accompanied by the masculine definite article. Take a look at the following chart.

	Singular	Plural
Masculine	el	los
Feminine	la	las

There is one exception to the rule. When the definite article comes before a feminine word that begins with *a* or *ha*, the singular masculine article is used. You can probably guess why if you say it out loud—Spanish will not accept the double "a" sound.

▶ el agua ⟶ las aguas *the water / the waters*
   NOT: la agua

▶ el águila ⟶ las águilas *the eagle / the eagles*
   NOT: la águila

Indefinite Articles

The indefinite articles *un*, *una*, *unos*, and *unas* (in additional to meaning "one") are equivalent to the English indefinite articles "a," "an," and "some." The indefinite article refers to something in general. For example, in "a house," "a" refers to a house in general.

In Spanish, indefinite articles follow the same rules as the definite articles.

	Singular	Plural
Masculine	uno	unos
Feminine	una	unas

Again, when the indefinite article comes before a feminine word that begins with *a* or *ha*, the singular masculine article is used.

un agua ⟶ unas aguas *a water / some waters*
un hacha ⟶ unas hachas *an axe / some axes*

LESSON 2

Present Tense of Ser

The verb "to be" is arguably the most important verb in English. This is also true of Spanish: there are few verbs that you will use more than *ser*. *Ser* is an irregular verb—in other words, its forms don't follow regular patterns.

ser (to be)		
Person	Singular	Plural
1st	yo **soy**	nosotros **somos**
2nd	tú **eres**	vosotros **sois**
3rd	él **es**	ellos **son**
	ella **es**	ellas **son**
	usted **es**	ustedes **son**

Use *ser* to:

▸ Identify people and things.

> José y Antonio **son** mis hermanos.   *José and Antonio are my brothers.*
> Mi número de teléfono **es** 555-1453.   *My phone number is 555-1453.*

▸ To express possession. Include *de.*

> El lapíz **es de** Jaime.   *The pencil is Jaime's.*

▸ To express origin. Include *de.*

> ¿**Eres de** Chile?   *You're from Chile?*

▸ To tell time.

> **Son** las tres y media.   *It's 3:30.*

Functional Language: Telling Time

Both English and Spanish use the verb "to be" to tell time. Spanish, however, uses both the singular and plural, depending on the hour.

"¿Qué hora es?" is used to ask "What time is it?" To answer this question, say

> **Es** la una.   *It's one o'clock.*
> **BUT**
> **Son** las dos.   *It's two o'clock.*

As seen in the examples, *es* is used with the singular hour, one. *Son* is used with all the other hours. Notice, too, how the definite article changes from *la* to *las*. Add *y* (and) to express the minutes.

Take a look at the following examples. Notice the alternate terminology.

LESSON 2

> **Es la** una **y cinco**.   *It's 1:05.* (literally, "It is the one and five")

> **Son las** siete **y treinta**.   *It's 7:30.* (literally, "It is the seven and thirty")
> **Son las** siete **y media**.   *It's 7:30.* (literally, "It is the seven and a half")

LESSON 2

Son las cuatro **y quince**.   *It is 4:15.*
(literally, "It is the four and fifteen")
Son las cuatro **y cuarto**.   *It is 4:15.*
(literally, "It is the four and a quarter")

Es mediodía.   *It is 12 noon.* (literally, "It is
midday")

Es medianoche.   *It is 12 at night.* (literally,
"It is midnight")

▶ After the half-hour, you can express the time
by subtracting minutes from the next hour.

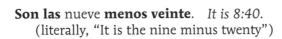

Son las nueve **menos veinte**.   *It is 8:40.*
(literally, "It is the nine minus twenty")

Son las seis **menos quince**.   *It is 5:45.*
(literally, "It is the six minus fifteen")
Son las seis **menos cuarto**.   *It is 5:45.*
(literally, "It is the six minus a
quarter.")

EXPRESSIONS OF TIME

Here are some words and phrases that will help you more accurately express the time.

▶ a las . . .   *at . . .*

  a las diez y media   *at 10:30*

▶ en punto   *sharp*

  a las seis en punto   *at six sharp*

▶ de la mañana   *in the morning, a.m.*

  a las nueve de la mañana   *at nine in the morning*

▶ de la tarde   *in the afternoon, p.m.*

  a las cinco de la tarde   *at 5 p.m.*

▶ de la noche   *in the evening, p.m.*

  a las diez de la noche   *at 10 p.m.*

PITFALL!   *Remember that* son las dos *means "it's 2 o'clock," while* a las dos *means "at 2 o'clock."*

Sample Test Questions

PART 1, Exercise A

Use what you've learned about gender to decide which definite article accompanies each noun. Write the article in the space provided.

1. _____ mano

2. _____ mesa

3. _____ piel

4. _____ personaje

5. _____ agua

6. _____ actriz

7. _____ niño

8. _____ rey

9. _____ hija

10. _____ artista

Exercise B

Change each definite article to an indefinite article. Rewrite the entire phrase in the space provided.

1. las nueces _____

2. el águila _____

3. los mapas _____

4. la pluma _____

5. las fotos _____

LESSON 2

Exercise C

Now change each indefinite article to a definite article. Rewrite the entire phrase in the space provided.

1. *un garaje* _____

2. *una decisión* _____

3. *unos relojes* _____

4. *un barril* _____

5. *unas motos* _____

PART 2, Exercise A

Match the answers to the simple mathematical equations. Write the letter in the space provided.

1. $2 + 4 =$ _____	a. siete
2. $1 - 1 =$ _____	b. catorce
3. $17 + 2 =$ _____	c. treinta
4. $11 - 2 =$ _____	d. seis
5. $4 + 10 =$ _____	e. diez
6. $5 + 2 =$ _____	f. nueve
7. _____ $- 2 = 8$	g. tres
8. $24 -$ _____ $= 21$	h. cero
9. $20 + 10 =$ _____	i. diecinueve
10. $13 - 1 =$ _____	j. doce

Exercise B

Express the time in full sentences. Write your answer in the space provided.

3:15 PM

1. _____

_____

_____

1:10 AM

2. _____

_____

_____

4:50 PM

3. _____

_____

_____

8:15 PM

4. _____

_____

_____

9:00 AM

5. _____

_____

_____

LESSON 2

3:15 PM

6. _____

_____

_____

2:00 PM

7. _____

_____

_____

11:00 AM

8. _____

_____

_____

12:00 PM

9. _____

_____

_____

12:00 AM

10. _____

_____

_____

LESSON 2

Lesson 3

Forming Sentences
- Sentence Components
- Subject and Predicate

Subject Pronouns
- *Vosotros*

Verbs: The Present Tense
- Present Tense of Regular Verbs: *-ar*
- Present Tense of Regular Verbs: *-er* and *-ir*

Subject-Verb Agreement

Functional Language: Questions
- Forming Questions

Sample Test Questions

3

Forming Sentences

In the first two lessons, we gave you just a taste of Spanish. Now let's start thinking in terms of meaningful communication. We'll begin with forming sentences.

SENTENCE COMPONENTS

Here are the basic components of a sentence and their functions. You will recognize some of these. Others you will learn about in later lessons. Take a look at the Table of Contents if you want to jump to them now.

▸ *Sustantivo* (noun): a person, place, thing, or idea

la <u>imaginación</u>   *the imagination*
los <u>estudiantes</u>   *the students*

▸ *Verbo* (verb): an action or state

pensar   *to think*
ser   *to be*

▸ *Artículo* (article): accompanies and identifies a noun

<u>el</u> libro   *the book*
<u>una</u> muñeca   *a doll*

▸ *Adjetivo* (adjective): modifies a noun

la silla <u>roja</u>   *the red chair*
el niño <u>travieso</u>   *the naughty boy*

▸ *Adverbio* (adverb): modifies a verb, adjective, or another adverb

Marta habla <u>bien</u>.   *Marta speaks well.*
La mujer camina <u>lentamente</u>.   *The woman walks slowly.*

▸ *Pronombre* (pronoun): replaces a noun

<u>Jorge</u> tiene 13 años. <u>Él</u> tiene 13 años.   *Jorge is 13 years old. He is 13 years old.*

▶ *Preposición* (preposition): expresses the relationship between things in terms of time or place

    El lápiz está <u>en</u> la mesa.   *The pencil is on the table.*
    Te veo <u>antes de</u> las 3:00.   *See you before 3:00.*

Now that we've reviewed the basics, let's learn how to form a complete sentence in Spanish.

SUBJECT AND PREDICATE

In Spanish, as in English, a sentence is formed by combining a subject and a verb, or predicate. The **subject** is the person or thing that we are talking about, generally a noun. The **predicate** is everything else. The predicate can describe a quality or an action. It contains the verb.

Take a look at the following sentences in English before you move on to the Spanish examples.

    subject   predicate
    <u>The cat</u> <u>is playing with the toy mouse</u>.

    subject   predicate
    <u>Teddy's mom</u> <u>is the school nurse</u>.

Now look at these sentences in Spanish. Try to identify the subjects and the predicates.

    Mi amigo Daniel está muy feliz.   *My friend Daniel is very happy.*
    Los muchachos están en la cocina.   *The boys are in the kitchen.*
    La hermana de Cristina es inteligente.   *Cristina's sister is intelligent.*

As you can see, both the subject and the predicate can contain more than one word. In the sentences, the subjects are *Mi amigo Daniel*, *Los muchachos*, and *La hermana de Cristina*. The predicates are *está muy contento*, *están en la cocina*, and *es inteligente*.

You can also see that in Spanish, the subject generally comes first, followed by the verb, and then the adjective or object (if there is one).

Subject Pronouns

Before we discuss regular Spanish verbs, let's review subject pronouns. A pronoun replaces a noun in a sentence. A **subject pronoun**, therefore, replaces a noun that is a subject.

Andrew likes hamburgers. **He** likes hamburgers.

Margaret and Suzy are going to the store. **They** are going to the store.

Here are the Spanish subject pronouns. You will see them throughout the rest of the book. Note that there is no equivalent for the English "it."

For the singular:

Person		
1st	yo	*I*
2nd	tú	*you*
3rd	él	*he*
	ella	*she*
	usted	*you* (formal)

Yo hablo español.   *I speak Spanish.*
Tú eres mi amigo.   *You are my friend.*
Ella es mi compañera.   *She is my classmate.*
Usted es muy alto.   *You are very tall.* **(formal)**

For the plural:

Person		
1st	nosotros	*we* (masculine)
	nosotras	*we* (feminine)
2nd	vosotros	*you* (plural, masculine)
	vosotras	*you* (plural, feminine)
3rd	ellos	*they* (masculine)
	ellas	*they* (feminine)
	ustedes	*you* (plural, formal)

Nosotros somos hermanos.   *We're brothers.*
Vosotros sois de España.   *You're from Spain.*
Ellas son de Bolivia.   *They're from Bolivia.*

VOSOTROS

You may or may not be tested on the *vosotros* form. If you plan on using your Spanish in Latin America, don't spend too much time worrying about it, because people there seldom use it. Use *ustedes* instead. If you are traveling in Spain, on the other hand, it would be wise to study the *vosotros* form. In any case, you should at least be able to recognize it.

Note: Spanish has four subject pronouns that mean "you."

▶ Use *tú* to address someone informally, such as a friend or someone younger.

▶ Use *usted* to address someone formally, such as a teacher, stranger, or older person.

▶ Use *ustedes* to address two or more people formally or informally in Latin America. Use *ustedes* to address two or more people formally in Spain.

▶ Use *vosotros/vosotras* to address two or more people informally in Spain.

Nosotros, vosotros, and *ellos* can refer to either a group of men or a group of men and women. *Nosotras, vosotras,* and *ellas* can refer only to a group of women.

> *Addressing People with Pronouns The rules regarding which pronouns to use to address people can vary enormously from country to country. To be safe, err on the side of formality and use usted and ustedes (better to be overly formal than overly familiar). When in doubt, ask the person how he or she wants to be addressed.*

Verbs: The Present Tense

A verb, as you've learned, is a word that expresses a state or action.

> Carol **eats** breakfast every day. (*eats* expresses an action)
> Daniel **is** in a good mood. (*is* expresses a state)

In Spanish, all verbs end with one of three letter combinations: *-ar*, *-er*, or *-ir*.

> cant**ar**   *to sing*
> com**er**   *to eat*
> escrib**ir**   *to write*

There are both regular and irregular verbs with all three endings. Regular verbs all conjugate in the same way. When you conjugate a verb, you form different tenses (past, present, future) and persons (I, you, he, she, it, we, they). Once you learn how to conjugate a regular verb, you can conjugate all verbs like it in the same way.

PRESENT TENSE OF REGULAR VERBS: -AR

In all regular Spanish verbs, the first section of the word, or stem, stays the same when conjugated.

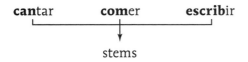

cantar   **com**er   **escrib**ir

stems

To form the present tense of a regular verb, first drop the infinitive ending: *-ar*, *-er*, *-ir*.

For singular *-ar* verbs, add *-o*, *-as*, or *-a*.

Person	Singular	
1st	yo canto	*I sing*
2nd	tú cantas	*you sing*
3rd	él canta	*he sings*
	ella canta	*she sings*
	usted canta	*you sing* (formal)

For plural -*ar* verbs, add -*amos*, -*áis*, or -*an*.

Person	Plural	
1st	nosotros cantamos	*we sing* (masculine)
	nosotras cantamos	*we sing* (feminine)
2nd	vosotros cantáis	*you sing* (plural, masculine)
	vosotras cantáis	*you sing* (plural, feminine)
3rd	ellos cantan	*they sing* (masculine)
	ellas cantan	*they sing* (feminine)
	ustedes cantan	*you sing* (plural, formal)

PRESENT TENSE OF REGULAR VERBS: -ER AND -IR

When conjugating singular -*er* verbs, add -*o*, -*es*, or -*e* to the verb stem.

Person	Singular	
1st	yo como	*I eat*
2nd	tú comes	*you eat*
3rd	él come	*he eats*
	ella come	*she eats*
	usted come	*you eat* (formal)

When conjugating plural -*er* verbs, add -*emos*, -*éis*, or -*en*.

Person	Plural	
1st	nosotros comemos	*we eat* (masculine)
	nosotras comemos	*we eat* (feminine)
2nd	vosotros coméis	*you eat* (plural, masculine)
	vosotras coméis	*you eat* (plural, feminine)
3rd	ellos comen	*they eat* (masculine)
	ellas comen	*they eat* (feminine)
	ustedes comen	*you eat* (plural, formal)

LESSON 3

When conjugating singular -*ir* verbs, add -*o*, -*es*, or -*e*.

Person	Singular	
1st	yo escribo	*I write*
2nd	tú escribes	*you write*
3rd	él escribe	*he writes*
	ella escribe	*she writes*
	usted escribe	*you write* (formal)

When conjugating plural -*ir* verbs, add -*imos*, -*ís*, or -*en*.

Person	Plural	
1st	nosotros escribimos	*we write* (masculine)
	nosotras escribimos	*we write* (feminine)
2nd	vosotros escribís	*you write* (plural, masculine)
	vosotras escribís	*you write* (plural, feminine)
3rd	ellos escriben	*they write* (masculine)
	ellas escriben	*they write* (feminine)
	ustedes escriben	*you write* (plural, formal)

Subject-Verb Agreement

In Spanish, each verb tense has a specific ending that agrees with the subject in person and in number. As you have seen, there are six possible endings for each verb—three singular and three plural.

Remember that the predicate is everything we say about the subject. The predicate must have at least one word. This word, a verb, should agree in person and number with the subject.

In this example, *canta* agrees in number with *Carla* (both are singular). The verb has to agree with the subject:

subject predicate
<u>Carla</u> <u>canta</u>.   *Carla sings.*

In the next example, *cantan* agrees in number with *Las niñas*. Both are plural.

subject   predicate
Las niñas cantan.   *The girls sing.*

Interestingly, a Spanish sentence can be made up of a single, conjugated verb because it includes both concepts: subject and predicate. Unlike English, Spanish verb endings are each unique. In other words, you can generally tell who the subject is by simply looking at the verb ending. The subject or subject pronoun is only used if there is ambiguity.

Canta.   *He/She sings.*
Cantamos.   *We sing.*

Functional Language: Questions

Now that you know how to form a sentence and how to conjugate regular verbs in the present tense, let's learn how to form a question.

FORMING QUESTIONS

There are several ways to form a question. One way is to add a tag at the end of the sentence. (The following English sentences have tags: "You're from Oregon, **right**?" "Francis likes asparagus, **no**?" "You'll be home by 10, **correct**?")

sentence: María habla español.   *María speaks Spanish.*
question: María habla español, ¿no?   *María speaks Spanish, doesn't she?*

Another way to ask a question is to invert, or switch the placement of, the subject and the verb. The word order will generally be: verb + rest of predicate (if any) + subject. Spanish is flexible: as long as the verb comes first, it generally doesn't matter which noun comes next.

LESSON 3

sentence: María habla español. *María speaks Spanish.*
question: ¿Habla español María? *Does María speak Spanish?*
also OK: ¿Habla María español?

A third way is to change the intonation of the sentence: simply make the sentence a question. However, this is the least common way of asking a question. Be careful if you choose to use it, because it can result in miscommunication.

sentence: María habla español. *María speaks Spanish.*
question: ¿María habla español? *María speaks Spanish?*

Question Words

Like in English, questions in Spanish often begin with question words. Here are some question words, or *palabras interrogativas.*

¿Qué?	*What?*	¿Cuándo?	*When?*
¿Quién?	*Who?*	¿Cuánto/a?	*How much?*
¿Quiénes?	*Who? (plural)*	¿Cuántos/as?	*How many?*
¿Cuál?	*Which one?*	¿Dónde?	*Where?*
¿Cuáles?	*Which ones?*	¿Adónde?	*To where?*
		¿De dónde?	*From where?*
¿Cómo?	*How?*	¿Por qué?	*Why?*

As a rule, all question words carry an accent mark on the stressed vowel.

Now take a look at how question words are used.

▶ **¿Qué** quieres? *What do you want?*

▶ **¿Quién** es? / **¿Quiénes** son? *Who is it? / Who are they?*

▶ **¿Cuál** es tu libro? *Which one is your book?*
  ¿Cuáles son tus libros? *Which ones are your books?*

▶ **¿Cómo** tomas el café? *How do you take your coffee?*

▶ **¿Cuándo** vamos al teatro? *When are we going to the theater?*

▸ ¿**Cuánta** leche quieres? *How much milk do you want?*
¿**Cuántas** manzanas quieres? *How many apples do you want?*

▸ ¿**Dónde** está el carro? *Where is the car?*

▸ ¿**Adónde** vas? *Where are you going?*

▸ ¿**De dónde** eres? *Where are you from?*

▸ ¿**Por qué** estudias el español? *Why do you study Spanish?*

Note: *¿Cuál?* and *¿Cuáles?* are often used to choose from among a group of things. For example, in the following sentences, it is assumed that there are several books to choose from.

¿**Cuál** es tu libro? *Which one is your book?*
¿**Cuáles** son tus libros? *Which ones are your books?*

PITFALL!   *¿Por qué? vs. Porque* ¿Por qué? means "Why?"
Porque means "because."

¿**Por qué** estudias tanto? *Why do you study so much?*
Porque quiero buenas notas. *Because I want good grades.*

Spanish Punctuation, Part 1 In Spanish, question marks (signos de interrogación) *and exclamation marks* (signos de exclamación) *are used at the beginning and the end of a question.*

¿Cuándo empieza el concierto? *When does the concert start?*

If a sentence contains more than a question, the question marks frame only the question.

Laura es argentina, ¿verdad? *Laura is Argentinean, right?*

Exclamation points (signos de exclamación) *are used in the same way as question marks.*

¡Estoy tan cansada! *I'm so tired!*
Si estás listo, ¡vámonos! *If you're ready, let's go!*

LESSON 3

Sample Test Questions

PART 1, Exercise A

Fill in the gaps with the correct verb form.

1. *saludar*   to greet

Person	Singular	Plural
1st	yo _____	nosotros _____
		nosotras saludamos
2nd	tú saludas	vosotros _____
		vosotras saludáis
3rd	él saluda	ellos saludan
	ella _____	ellas _____
	usted saluda	ustedes saludan

2. _____   to learn

Person	Singular	Plural
1st	yo aprendo	nosotros aprendemos
		nosotras _____
2nd	tú _____	vosotros _____
		vosotras aprendéis
3rd	él _____	ellos _____
	ella _____	ellas aprenden
	usted aprende	ustedes _____

Exercise B

Fill in the blanks with the correct form of the verb in parentheses.

1. Iris _____ (correr) en el parque.

2. Mis hermanas _____ (vivir) en Nueva York.

3. Yo _____ (abrir) el libro.

4. Vosotras _____ (estudiar) el español.

5. Tú _____ (comer) una pera.

6. Nosotros _____ (preparar) la comida.

7. Usted _____ (leer) la revista.

8. Ustedes _____ (escribir) una carta.

9. Yo _____ (comprender) el ejercicio.

10. Vosotros _____ (regresar) a casa.

Exercise C

Read the following sentences. Do they show subject-verb agreement? If they don't, correct the errors by rewriting the sentences.

1. Martín regresa a España.

   _____

2. Tú prepara la tarea.

   _____

3. Yo como el pan.

   _____

4. *Vosotros viven en los Estados Unidos.*

_____

5. *Miguel estudian el inglés.*

_____

PART 2, Exercise A

Translate the following into Spanish. If you don't know a word, look it up in the dictionary.

1. 65 _____

2. 31 _____

3. 100 _____

4. 82 _____

5. 50 _____

Exercise B

Invert the subjects and verbs to create questions. Write the questions on the lines provided.

1. *Jorge estudia en la universidad.*

   _____

2. *Ella canta.*

   _____

3. *Los profesores son buenos.*

   _____

4. *Iris tiene 19 años.*

   _____

5. *Tú eres de Guatemala.*

   _____

Exercise C

Fill in the blank with the correct question word. Write the word in the space provided.

   cuándo   dónde   cuánta   quién   cuántos

1. ¿_____ *años tienes?*

2. *¿De* _____ *eres?*

3. ¿_____ *es tu profesor de español?*

4. ¿_____ *leche* (milk) *quieres en tu café?*

5. ¿_____ *empieza* (begins) *la clase?*

Lesson 4

Descriptive Adjectives
- Adjective-Noun Agreement
- Long and Short Adjectives
- Adjective Placement

Possessive Adjectives
- Short Possessive Adjectives
- Long Possessive Adjectives

Estar vs. *Ser*
- *Estar*
- *Ser* as an Equation
- *Ser* and *Estar* with Adjectives
- Changes in Meaning

Demonstrative Adjectives
- Close to the Speaker
- Close to the Listener
- Far from Both Speakers

Numbers 101 and Higher

Functional Language: Answering Questions

Sample Test Questions

4

Descriptive Adjectives

In Lesson 3 we briefly discussed adjectives. Adjectives describe nouns. There are many kinds of adjectives, including descriptive adjectives, possessive adjectives, and demonstrative adjectives. Let's look at descriptive adjectives first.

A **descriptive adjective** describes a person, place, or thing.

> la silla **roja**   *the red chair*
> el niño **bueno**   *the good boy*

The adjectives *roja* and *bueno* modify the nouns *silla* and *niño*.

> **Adjectives to Describe People** *In Spanish, unlike English, it is often acceptable to refer to a person informally by a physical characteristic. Sometimes the references are true, but often they are not. Ironically, the nicknames* el flaco, la gorda, el viejo, *and such can be given to people who do not have these attributes (e.g., a young person can be called* el viejo).

ADJECTIVE-NOUN AGREEMENT

You've already learned that verbs need to agree in number and person with their subjects. Adjectives, too, must agree with the nouns they modify. They should agree with them in both gender and number.

Adjective-Noun Agreement: Gender

▸ If the noun is masculine, the adjective must be masculine too. If the noun is feminine, the adjective must be feminine. Usually, masculine adjectives end in *-o* and feminine adjectives end in *-a*. Take a look at these examples.

> **el** libr**o** viej**o**   *the old book*
> **la** cas**a** viej**a**   *the old house*

▶ Some adjectives don't end in -a or -o. These adjectives generally can modify either feminine or masculine nouns.

la tarea fác**il**   *the easy homework*
el ejercicio fác**il**   *the easy exercise*

▶ Masculine adjectives that end in -or can be made feminine by adding -a.

un hombre hablad**or**   *a talkative man*
una mujer hablad**ora**   *a talkative woman*

un hombre trabajad**or**   *a hardworking man*
una mujer trabajad**ora**   *a hardworking woman*

Adjective-Noun Agreement: Number

▶ If a noun is plural, its accompanying adjective should be plural too. To form the plural, add -s to an adjective that ends with a vowel.

los libr**os** viej**os**   *the old books*
las cas**as** viej**as**   *the old houses*

▶ Add -es to an adjective that ends with a consonant.

los hombres jóven**es**   *the young man*
las mujeres jóven**es**   *the young woman*

▶ If an adjective ends with a -z, change the -z to a -c and add -es.

el niño feli**z**   *the happy boy*
los niños feli**ces**   *the happy boys*

Note: As with subject pronouns, use the masculine plural ending to describe a mixed group of masculine and female nouns.

los niñ**os** traviesos   *the naughty children*
          ↓
niños/niñas OR niños

las niñ**as** traveies**as**   *the naughty girls*

↓

niñas

LONG AND SHORT ADJECTIVES

Some descriptive adjectives have both long and short versions.

▶ Some adjectives drop their final -*o* when they come before a singular, masculine noun. Take a look at these examples.

un libro **bueno** ⟶ un **buen** libro   *a good book*

Other words like *bueno*:

alguno   *some*
malo   *bad*
primero   *first*

▶ *Grande* becomes *gran* in front of any singular noun. However, the meaning changes.

un evento **grande** *(a big event)* ⟶ un **gran** evento
  a great event

> **PITFALL!**   *Be careful with* grande *and* gran—*if you say,* Es una gran mujer, *you're saying "She's a great woman," which is a nice compliment. However, if you say,* Es una mujer grande, *you're saying "She's a big woman," which isn't so nice.*

▶ *Santo* becomes *San* in front of any masculine name, unless that name begins with *To-* or *Do-*.

San Nicolás
San Francisco

Santo Tomás
Santo Domingo

ADJECTIVE PLACEMENT

▸ Descriptive adjectives like *guapo* (good-looking), *hermoso* (beautiful), and *delgado* (thin) usually come after the nouns they describe.

> una actor **guapo**   *a good-looking actor*
> una actriz **hermosa**   *a beautiful actress*

▸ Adjectives that indicate a number or quantity usually go before the nouns they describe.

> **algunos** actores guapos   *some good-looking actors*
> **muchas** actrices hermosas   *many beautiful actresses*

Other words like *algunos* and *muchas*:

> ningún   *no, not any*
> varios   *various*

> **PITFALL!**   Ningún/ninguna *is always singular.*

▸ As we explained in the previous section, some adjectives change meaning depending on where they're placed. *Gran* and *grande* are two examples. Other examples are:

> un **viejo** amigo (*a longtime friend*) ⟶ un amigo **viejo** *an elderly friend*
> una mujer **pobre** (*a woman with no money*) ⟶ una **pobre** mujer   *a pitiful woman*

Possessive Adjectives

Adjectives don't only have to be descriptive. **Possessive adjectives**, as their name suggests, indicate possession. Like all adjectives, they agree with the nouns they describe.

SHORT POSSESSIVE ADJECTIVES

Possessive adjectives can be short or long. These are the short possessive adjectives.

For a singular noun:

Person	Singular	
1st	mi mochila/libro	*my backpack/book*
2nd	tu mochila/libro	*your backpack/book*
3rd	su mochila/libro	*his, her, its, your* (formal) *backpack/ book*

Person	Plural	
1st	nuestra mochila nuestro libro	*our backpack/book*
2nd	vuestra mochila vuestro libro	*your* (plural) *backpack/book*
3rd	su mochila su libro	*their, your* (plural, formal) *backpack/ book*

For a plural noun:

Person	Singular	
1st	mis mochilas/libros	*my backpacks/books*
2nd	tus mochilas/libros	*your backpacks/books*
3rd	sus mochilas/libros	*his, her, its, your* (formal) *backpacks/ books*

Person	Plural	
1st	nuestras mochilas nuestros libros	*our backpacks/books*
2nd	vuestras mochilas vuestros libros	*your* (plural) *backpacks/books*
3rd	sus mochilas sus libros	*their, your* (plural, formal) *backpacks/ books*

▶ Short possessive adjectives always come before the nouns they modify.

Mi carro es viejo.   *My car is old.*
No tengo **mis** libros hoy.   *I don't have my books today.*

LONG POSSESSIVE ADJECTIVES

Long possessive adjectives always follow the noun they describe.

For a singular noun:

Person	Singular	
1st	mío/mía	*of mine*
2nd	tuyo/tuya	*of yours*
3rd	suyo/suya	*of his, hers, its, yours* (formal)
Person	**Plural**	
1st	nuestro/nuestra	*of ours*
2nd	vuestra/vuestro	*of yours* (plural)
3rd	suyo/suya	*of theirs, yours* (plural, formal)

For a plural noun:

Person	Singular	
1st	míos/mías	*of mine*
2nd	tuyos/tuyas	*of yours*
3rd	suyos/suyas	*of his, hers, its, yours* (formal)
Person	**Plural**	
1st	nuestros/nuestras	*of ours*
2nd	vuestras/vuestros	*of yours* (plural)
3rd	suyos/suyas	*of theirs, yours* (plural, formal)

▶ Use long possessive adjectives when you would say "of . . . " in English.

  Es una amiga **mía**.   *She is a friend of mine.*

▶ You can also use long possessive adjectives after the verb *ser*.

  La caja es **nuestra**.   *The box is ours.*

PITFALL!	In Spanish, the possessive adjectives agree in gender and number with the thing possessed, not with the possessor.

Estar vs. Ser

In Lesson 2, we learned how to conjugate the verb *ser*. Before we move on to demonstrative adjectives, let's discuss the verb *estar*, the other "to be" verb. Notice the irregular conjugation. We will learn more about irregular verbs in Lesson 5. We will learn more about *ser* and *estar* in Lesson 6.

ESTAR

estar (to be)		
Person	Singular	Plural
1st	yo **estoy**	nosotros **estamos**
2nd	tú **estás**	vosotros **estáis**
3rd	él **está**	ellos **están**
	ella **está**	ellas **están**
	usted **está**	ustedes **están**

If both *ser* and *estar* mean "to be," then how do you use these verbs?

SER AS AN EQUATION

▸ Think of the verb *ser* as an equal sign (=). You remember from math that the items on either side of an equal sign must, by definition, be the same. The verb *ser* is equivalent to an equal sign. It links two elements that are grammatically similar. For example, *ser* can link two nouns, two infinitive verbs, or a pronoun and a noun. Look at the following examples.

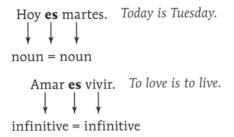

Hoy **es** martes.   *Today is Tuesday.*

noun = noun

Amar **es** vivir.   *To love is to live.*

infinitive = infinitive

Yo **soy** estudiante.   *I am a student.*

↓   ↓   ↓

pronoun = noun

▶ *Ser* can also express place of origin (nationality), when used with *de.*

Soy de Guatemala.   *I'm from Guatemala.*

Days of the Week

Note that the names are not capitalized.

Monday: lunes   **Tuesday:** martes   **Wednesday:** miércoles
Thursday: jueves   **Friday:** viernes   **Saturday:** sábado
Sunday: domingo

Prepositions with Days of the Week
If you want to say "on Monday," use el: el lunes.

El lunes voy a la biblioteca.   *On Monday I'm going to the library.*

If you want to say, "on Mondays," use los: los lunes.

Los lunes voy a la biblioteca.   *On Mondays I go to the library.*

SER AND ESTAR WITH ADJECTIVES

▶ Use *ser* to express qualities that are unlikely to change. For example, use *ser* with adjectives of nationality, size, or color. Look at the following examples.

Soy ecuatoriana.   *I am Ecuadorian.*
Las manzanas **son** rojas.   *The apples are red.*
La pelota **es** redonda.   *The ball is round.*

▶ Use *ser* with adjectives that describe personal qualities too.

Miguel **es** alto.   *Miguel is tall.*
Mi hermana **es** simpática.   *My sister is nice.*

▶ Use *estar* to describe temporary qualities or conditions that are likely to change.

> **Estoy** cansado.   *I'm tired.*
> Mauricio **está** nervioso.   *Mauricio is nervous.*

By using the verb *estar*, it is implied that the person in the first sentence will not always be tired and the person in the second sentence will not always be nervous.

Think about the example *Las manzanas son rojas*. What if you were to replace *son* with *están*? *Las manzanas están rojas* implies that at one point the apples were not red or that they will not always be red. Look at the following sentences.

> ¡**Eres** bella, Margarita!
> ¡**Estás** bella, Margarita!

Can you tell what the difference is? *¡Eres bella, Margarita!* means "You're beautiful, Margarita!" *¡Estás bella, Margarita!*, on the other hand, means "You look beautiful, Margarita," or, "You're beautiful (right now) Margarita."

What about the other example, *Miguel es alto*? If you said, *Miguel está alto*, that would imply that he has changed height since the last time you saw him. Perhaps he was a little boy who grew up, or perhaps he works at a circus and wears stilts. Both of these possibilities are pretty remote, so consider that when you're deciding which verb is appropriate.

CHANGES IN MEANING

Some adjectives may change meaning depending on which verb is used: *ser* or *estar*. Take a look at these examples.

▶ aburrido (boring vs. bored):

> Esa profesora **es** aburrida.   *That professor is boring.*
> Esa profesorsa **está** aburrida.   *That professor is bored.*

▶ bueno (good vs. tasty):

> La fruta **es** buena para la salud.   *Fruit is good for your health.*
> La fruta **está** buena.   *Fruit is tasty.*

▶ cómodo (comfortable object vs. comfortable person):

> La silla **es** cómoda.   *The chair is comfortable.*
> **Estoy** cómodo.   *I'm comfortable.*

▶ rico (wealthy vs. tasty):

> Mi tío **es** rico.   *My uncle is wealthy.*
> El pollo **está** rico.   *The chicken is good.*

Note: See Lesson 6 for more on *ser* vs. *estar*.

Demonstrative Adjectives

Demonstrative adjectives are another kind of adjective. They distinguish one group of items from another. Demonstrative adjectives in Spanish are equivalent to the English words "this," "that," "these," and "those." They also agree with the nouns they accompany.

In Spanish, demonstrative adjectives change depending on the location of the object that the speaker is talking about.

CLOSE TO THE SPEAKER

Some demonstrative adjectives refer to something that is close to the speaker. Like all adjectives, they must agree in number and gender with the noun they describe.

Singular

este libro	*this book*
esta pluma	*this pen*

Plural

estos libr**os**	*these books*
estas plum**as**	*these pens*

¿Quieres **este** libro, o **estas** plumas?   *Do you want this book or these pens?*

CLOSE TO THE LISTENER

Some demonstrative adjectives refer to something that is close to the listener.

Singular

ese libr**o**	*that pen*
esa plum**a**	*that book*

Plural

esos libr**os**	*those books*
esas plum**as**	*those pens*

¿Quieres **esa** camisa, o **esos** pantalones?   *Do you want that shirt or those pants?*

FAR FROM BOTH SPEAKERS

Other demonstrative adjectives refer to something that is far from both the speaker and listener.

Singular

aquel libro	*that book*
aquella pluma	*that pen*

Plural

aquellos libros	*those books*
aquellas plumas	*those pens*

> ¿Ves **aquel** pájaro? ¿Ves **aquellos** patos? *Can you see that bird? Can you see those ducks?*

Numbers 101 and Higher

Before we introduce the functional language topic of this lesson, let's learn some more numbers in Spanish.

101	ciento uno/una	800	ochocientos/as
200	doscientos/as	900	novecientos/as
300	trescientos/as	1.000	mil
400	cuatrocientos/as	2.000	dos mil
500	quinientos/as	1.000.000	un millón (de)
600	seiscientos/as	2.000.000	dos millones (de)
700	setecientos/as		

Spanish Punctuation, Part 2 *Spanish uses periods to indicate thousands (and millions).*

> 1.100 hormigas   *1,100 ants*

Spanish also uses commas to indicate decimals.

> 1.342,30 dólares   *1,342.30 dollars*

▶ When the numbers 200–900 modify a noun, then need to agree in gender.

> quinient**os** alumn**os**   *500 pupils*
> trescient**os** cincuenta niños   *350 boys*

▶ *Mil* means both "one thousand" and simply "thousand." It is invariable, even when used to describe multiple thousands.

> **mil** centavos   *1,000 cents*
> **dos mil** canciones   *2,000 songs*

▶ *Un millón* ("a million" or "one million") is used in both the singular and the plural. Notice that when *millón* comes before a noun, it needs to be accompanied by *de*.

> **un millón de** dólares   *1,000,000 dollars*
> **dos millones de** habitantes   *2,000,000 inhabitants*

PITFALL!   *To say "one thousand," use* mil *alone, not* un mil.

Functional Language: Answering Questions

In Lesson 3, we learned how to ask a question. Now we will discuss how to answer one.

▶ If the question asked is a yes/no question, such as:

¿Vas al cine? *Are you going to the cinema?*

Answer in the following ways:

Sí, voy. *Yes, I am going.*
No, no voy. *No, I'm not going.*

▶ When a question contains a question word, such as:

¿Cuándo es la fiesta? *When is the party?*
¿Por qué estás triste? *Why are you sad?*
¿Quién es? *Who is it?*

Answer in the following ways:

Es a las 5:00. *It's at 5:00.*
Porque no tengo amigos. *Because I don't have any friends.*
Es mi madre. *It's my mother.*

When answering questions, pay attention to the verb form. The verb form in the answer will be based on the one in the question. If the question is asked of *you*, for example, the answer is in the *I* form. If the question is asked about *him*, the answer is about *him*. Here are some rules.

▶ If the question is about *yo*, answer it with *tú* or *usted*.

¿Cuándo voy al colegio? *When am I going to school?*
Vas a las 8:00. *You're going at 8:00.*

▶ If the question is about *tú* or *usted*, answer it with *yo*.

¿Cuándo va usted al colegio? *When are you going to school?*
Voy a las 8:00. *I'm going at 8:00.*

▶ If the question is about *nosotros*, answer it with *nosotros*.

    ¿Cuándo vamos al colegio?   *When are we going to school?*
    Vamos a las 8:00.   *We're going at 8:00.*

▶ If the question is about *ellos*, answer it with *ellos*.

    ¿Cuándo van al colegio?   *When are they going to school?*
    Van a las 8:00.   *They're going at 8:00.*

▶ Finally, if the question is about *ustedes*, answer it with *nosotros*.

    ¿Cuándo van ustedes al colegio?   *When are you going
      to school?*
    Vamos a las 8:00.   *We're going at 8:00.*

Sample Test Questions

PART 1, Exercise A

Fill in the blank with the correct form of the adjective in parentheses.

1. *unas muchachas* _____ *(guapo)*

2. *un hombre* _____ *(joven)*

3. *unos libros* _____ *(bueno)*

4. *una mesa* _____ *(viejo)*

5. *un niño* _____ *(feliz)*

Exercise B

Choose the correct possessive adjective. Circle the answer.

1. _____ *hermana es Catalina.*
   - A. Tu
   - B. Tuya

2. *El lápiz es* _____ .
   - A. suyo
   - B. su

3. _____ *clase de matemáticas es difícil* (difficult).
   - A. Mía
   - B. Mi

4. _____ *profesora es muy* (very) *severa* (strict).
   - A. Nuestro
   - B. Nuestra

5. _____ *madre te espera* (is waiting for you).
   - A. Tu
   - B. Tuya

Exercise C

Unscramble the following sentences. Pay attention to adjective placement. Some sentences may have more than one answer.

1. *carro tengo un nuevo*

    _____

2. *grande perro ese es*

    _____

3. *es Emilia hermosa*

    _____

4. *mochilas vuestras esas son*

    _____

5. *¿tuyo aquel libro es?*

    _____

PART 2, Exercise A

Fill in the blank with the correct form of *ser* or *estar*.

1. *Yo _____ de Asunción, Paraguay.*

2. *Hay un examen a las 2. ¡Manuela _____ nerviosa!*

3. *El círculo _____ redondo.*

4. *Hoy Laura _____ de mal humor (in a bad mood).*

5. *Mi padre _____ alto y simpático.*

Exercise B

Choose the correct question to agree with each answer. Write the letter in the space provided.

1. _____ *Sí, hablo español.*

    A. ¿Quién habla español?
    B. ¿Hablas español?

2. _____ *No, Alberto no está aquí.*

    A. ¿Dónde está Alberto?
    B. Alberto no está aquí, ¿verdad?

3. _____ *Soy de Nueva York.*

    A. ¿De dónde es usted?
    B. ¿De dónde es Raúl?

4. _____ *Necesito (I need) un lápiz.*

    A. ¿Cuáles lapices necesitas?
    B. ¿Qué necesitas?

5. _____ *Porque es mi amiga.*

    A. ¿Dónde está Marta?
    B. ¿Por que hablas con Marta?

Exercise C

Add the following numbers. Write out the answers. Be sure that the numbers agree in gender with the nouns they modify.

1. *100 + 1.000 niñas =*

    _____

2. *2.000.000 + 500 + 20 insectos =*

    _____

LESSON 4

3. *1.500 + 500 libros =*

_____

4. *500 + 100 escuelas =*

_____

5. *1.000 + 300 + 10 señores =*

_____

Lesson 5

Present Tense of Stem-Changing Verbs
- e → ie
- e → i
- o → ue
- u → ue

Present Tense of *-uir*, *-iar*, and *-uar* Verbs
- *-uir* Verbs
- *-iar* and *-uar* Verbs

Present Tense of Verbs with Irregular *Yo* Forms
- *-go* Verbs
- *-zco* Verbs
- *-oy* Verbs

Functional Language: Using the Present Progressive
- The Present Progressive: Stem-Changing Verbs

Sample Test Questions

Present Tense of Stem-Changing Verbs

In addition to regular *-ar*, *-er*, and *-ir* verbs, Spanish has **stem-changing verbs**. Stem-changing verbs are different from regular verbs because when they are conjugated, they undergo spelling changes that follow regular patterns. This happens in all forms except *nosotros* and *vosotros*. Luckily, the endings are all regular, so you can still apply the endings that you learned in Lesson 3.

> **Verb Stems** Remember that a verb stem *is the root part of the verb that does not include the -ar/-er/-ir ending.*
> *For example:* cant*ar*, com*er*, escrib*ir*

There are several types of stem-changing verbs: *e* → *ie*, *e* → *i*, and *o* → *ue*, and *u* → *ue*. Take a look at the following examples.

E → IE

cerrar (to close)		
Person	Singular	Plural
1st	yo c**ie**rro	nosotros cerramos
2nd	tú c**ie**rras	vosotros cerráis
3rd	él c**ie**rra	ellos c**ie**rran
	ella c**ie**rra	ellas c**ie**rran
	usted c**ie**rra	ustedes c**ie**rran

> **Pensar** Pensar + *infinitive means to plan to do something.*
> Pensar + en *means to think about something or someone.*
>
> **¿Piensas ir** a clase hoy? *Do you think you'll go to class today?*
> **Pienso en** tí todos los días. *I think about you every day.*

perder (to lose)		
Person	**Singular**	**Plural**
1st	yo p**ie**rdo	nosotros perdemos
2nd	tú p**ie**rdes	vosotros perdéis
3rd	él p**ie**rde	ellos p**ie**rden
	ella p**ie**rde	ellas p**ie**rden
	usted p**ie**rde	ustedes p**ie**rden

Perder Perder *can also mean "to miss," as in, "to miss the bus."*

No quiero perder el bus. *I don't want to miss the bus.*

Other *e* → *ie* verbs like *cerrar* and *perder*:

defender *to defend*
despertar *to awaken*
empezar *to begin*
entender *to understand*
pensar *to think*
querer *to want / love*

sentir (to feel)		
Person	**Singular**	**Plural**
1st	yo s**ie**nto	nosotros sentimos
2nd	tú s**ie**ntes	vosotros sentís
3rd	él s**ie**nte	ellos s**ie**nten
	ella s**ie**nte	ellas s**ie**nten
	usted s**ie**nte	ustedes s**ie**nten

Other verbs like *sentir*:

mentir *to lie*
divertir *to amuse*
preferir *to prefer*

E → I

pedir (to request/ask)		
Person	Singular	Plural
1st	yo pido	nosotros pedimos
2nd	tú pides	vosotros pedís
3rd	él pide	ellos piden
	ella pide	ellas piden
	usted pide	ustedes piden

Preguntar and Pedir Preguntar *means to ask a question.* Pedir *means to ask for something.*

Other verbs like *pedir*:

repetir   *to repeat*
servir   *to serve*
vestir   *to dress*

O → UE

contar (to count/tell)		
Person	Singular	Plural
1st	yo **cue**nto	nosotros contamos
2nd	tú **cue**ntas	vosotros contáis
3rd	él **cue**nta	ellos **cue**ntan
	ella **cue**nta	ellas **cue**ntan
	usted **cue**nta	ustedes **cue**ntan

Other verbs like *contar*:

almorzar   *to have lunch*
costar   *to cost*
recordar   *to remember*

LESSON 5

volver (to return)		
Person	**Singular**	**Plural**
1st	yo v**ue**lvo	nosotros volvemos
2nd	tú v**ue**lves	vosotros volvéis
3rd	él v**ue**lve	ellos v**ue**lven
	ella v**ue**lve	ellas v**ue**lven
	usted v**ue**lve	ustedes v**ue**lven

Other verbs like *volver*:

> devolver   *to return*
> llover   *to rain*
> mover   *to move*

U → UE

jugar (to play)		
Person	**Singular**	**Plural**
1st	yo j**ue**go	nosotros jugamos
2nd	tú j**ue**gas	vosotros jugáis
3rd	él j**ue**ga	ellos j**ue**gan
	ella j**ue**ga	ellas j**ue**gan
	usted j**ue**ga	ustedes j**ue**gan

Jugar is the only verb with a stem change from *u* to *ue*. When you're talking about sports, use the following expression:

> **jugar + a** + [definite article] + sport
> Nosotros jugamos al fútbol.   *We play soccer.*

Present Tense of -uir, -iar, and -uar Verbs

There are three more kinds of regular verbs that have slight changes when conjugated: *-uir*, *-iar*, and *-uar* verbs.

-UIR VERBS

Verbs ending in -uir have a slight change in spelling when conjugated in all forms except *nosotros* and *vosotros*: when conjugating the verb, change the *i* to *y*.

Examine the following chart.

incluir (to include)		
Person	**Singular**	**Plural**
1st	yo inclu**y**o	nosotros incluimos
2nd	tú inclu**y**es	vosotros incluís
3rd	él inclu**y**e	ellos inclu**y**en
	ella inclu**y**e	ellas inclu**y**en
	usted inclu**y**e	ustedes inclu**y**en

Other verbs like *incluir*:

destruir *to destroy*
distribuir *to distribute*

-IAR AND -UAR VERBS

Verbs ending in -iar and -uar don't show spelling changes when conjugated. The change is a matter of stress.

When you conjugate -iar verbs, stress the *i* in the singular and third-person plural. Take a look at the following chart.

enviar (to send)		
Person	**Singular**	**Plural**
1st	yo envío	nosotros enviamos
2nd	tú envías	vosotros enviáis
3rd	él envía	ellos envían
	ella envía	ellas envían
	usted envía	ustedes envían

Other verbs like *enviar*:

confiar *to trust*
guiar *to guide*

When you conjugate *-uar* verbs, stress the *u* in the singular and third-person plural. Take a look at the following chart.

actuar (to act)		
Person	Singular	Plural
1st	yo actúo	nosotros actuamos
2nd	tú actúas	vosotros actuáis
3rd	él actúa	ellos actúan
	ella actúa	ellas actúan
	usted actúa	ustedes actúan

Other verbs like *actuar*:

continuar   *to continue*
graduarse   *to graduate*

Present Tense of Verbs with Irregular Yo Forms

Some Spanish verbs are irregular in the *yo* form of the present tense. Otherwise, they are regular. Take a look at the following charts.

-GO VERBS

hacer (to do, make)		
Person	Singular	Plural
1st	yo **hago**	nosotros hacemos
2nd	tú haces	vosotros hacéis
3rd	él hace	ellos hacen
	ella hace	ellas hacen
	usted hace	ustedes hacen

Notice how the only spelling change occurs in the *yo* form. All other forms are regular.

LESSON 5

Hacer and the Weather Use the verb hacer to talk about the weather.

¿Qué tiempo **hace**?   *What's the weather like?*
Hace sol.   *It's sunny.*
Hace calor.   *It's hot.*
Hace frío.   *It's cold.*
Hace viento.   *It's windy.*

poner (to put)		
Person	Singular	Plural
1st	yo **pongo**	nosotros ponemos
2nd	tú pones	vosotros ponéis
3rd	él pone	ellos ponen
	ella pone	ellas ponen
	usted pone	ustedes ponen

salir (to go out)		
Person	Singular	Plural
1st	yo **salgo**	nosotros salimos
2nd	tú sales	vosotros salís
3rd	él sale	ellos salen
	ella sale	ellas salen
	usted sale	ustedes salen

Salir To say you're going out with someone, use salir con. To say you're leaving a place, use salir de. To express your destination, use salir para.

María **sale con** Francisco.   *María is going out with Francisco.*
Jaime **sale del** cine.   *Jaime is leaving the cinema.*
Mañana **salgo para** Italia.   *Tomorrow I leave for Italy.*

The following *-go* verbs have both an irregular first-person singular conjugation and a stem change.

decir (to say)		
Person	**Singular**	**Plural**
1st	yo **digo**	nosotros decimos
2nd	tú dices	vosotros decís
3rd	él dice	ellos dicen
	ella dice	ellas dicen
	usted dice	ustedes dicen

tener (to have)		
Person	**Singular**	**Plural**
1st	yo **tengo**	nosotros tenemos
2nd	tú **tie**nes	vosotros tenéis
3rd	él **tie**ne	ellos **tie**nen
	ella **tie**ne	ellas **tie**nen
	usted **tie**ne	ustedes **tie**nen

venir (to come)		
Person	**Singular**	**Plural**
1st	yo **vengo**	nosotros venimos
2nd	tú **vie**nes	vosotros venís
3rd	él **vie**ne	ellos **vie**nen
	ella **vie**ne	ellas **vie**nen
	usted **vie**ne	ustedes **vie**nen

LESSON 5

Idiomatic Expressions with Tener

Tener is used in many Spanish idioms. Here are some of them.

▸ **tener . . . años**   *to be . . . years old*

Juan Martín tiene siete años.   *Juan Martín is seven years old.*

▸ **tener ganas de**   *to feel like*

¿Tienes ganas de ir al cine?   *Do you feel like going to the movies?*

▶ **tener miedo de**   *to be afraid of*

Tengo miedo de los ratones.   *I'm afraid of mice.*

▶ **tener prisa**   *to be in a hurry*

¡Vamos! Tengo prisa.   *Let's go! I'm in a hurry.*

▶ **tener que**   *to have to*

Tenemos que hacer las tareas.   *We have to do our homework.*

▶ **(no) tener razón**   *to be right/wrong*

Tienes razón: Marta es cubana.   *You're right: Marta is Cuban.*

▶ **tener sueño**   *to be sleepy*

El bebé tiene sueño.   *The baby is sleepy.*

▶ **tener hambre**   *to be hungry*

Margarita tiene hambre.   *Margarita is hungry.*

▶ **tener sed**   *to be thirsty*

Tengo sed. Quiero agua.   *I'm thirsty. I want water.*

-ZCO VERBS

As with the verbs previously discussed, verbs in this category feature a spelling change in the *yo* form only, but here they change from *c* to *zco*.

conocer (to know)		
Person	**Singular**	**Plural**
1st	yo **conozco**	nosotros conocemos
2nd	tú conoces	vosotros conocéis
3rd	él conoce	ellos conocen
	ella conoce	ellas conocen
	usted conoce	ustedes conocen

parecer (to appear/to seem)		
Person	**Singular**	**Plural**
1st	yo **parezco**	nosotros parecemos
2nd	tú pareces	vosotros parecéis
3rd	él parece	ellos parecen
	ella parece	ellas parecen
	usted parece	ustedes parecen

-OY VERBS

These verbs add a *-oy* to the *yo* form. The remaining conjugations are all regular.

dar (to give)		
Person	**Singular**	**Plural**
1st	yo **doy**	nosotros damos
2nd	tú das	vosotros dais
3rd	él da	ellos dan
	ella da	ellas dan
	usted da	ustedes dan

Functional Language: Using the Present Progressive

In English, you use "to be" and the present participle (the *-ing* form) to express an action that is in progress. Spanish has a similar construction: the **present progressive**.

The present progressive is formed with the present tense of *estar*, plus the present participle.

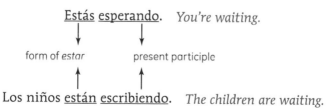

Estás esperando. *You're waiting.*

form of *estar*   present participle

Los niños están escribiendo. *The children are waiting.*

To form the present participle, drop the -ar, -er, or -ir ending of the verb and add the following:

▶ for -ar verbs ⟶ -ando

esper**ando**   *waiting*
jug**ando**   *playing*

▶ for -er verbs ⟶ -iendo

escrib**iendo**   *writing*
corr**iendo**   *running*

▶ for -ir verbs ⟶ -iendo

escrib**iendo**   *writing*
decid**iendo**   *deciding*

When the stem of an -er or -ir verb ends in a vowel, the present participle ends in -yendo.

leer ⟶ leyendo
traer ⟶ trayendo

Bear in mind that the present progressive in Spanish is used *only* to emphasize an action that is in progress at the time the speaker is talking.

> **PITFALL!**   *Unlike English, the present progressive does not talk about an action that will be occurring in the future. For example, "Mateo is going to Europe tomorrow" would be translated as* Mateo va a Europa mañana.

THE PRESENT PROGRESSIVE: STEM-CHANGING VERBS

Many -ir verbs have irregular present participles. Look out for the following:

▶ verbs that have a stem change from *e* ⟶ *i* in the present tense

pedir ⟶ pidiendo
seguir ⟶ siguiendo

▶ verbs that have a stem change from *e* → *ie* in the present tense

    sentir ──→ sintiendo
    preferir ──→ prefiriendo

▶ verbs that have a stem change from *o* → *ue* in the present tense

    dormir ──→ durmiendo

The Present Progressive and the Weather As in English, you can use the present progressive to talk about the weather.

    Está lloviendo.   *It's raining.*
    Está nevando.   *It's snowing.*

Sample Test Questions

PART 1, Exercise A

Match the subject pronouns with the appropriate conjugations. Write the letter in the blank.

1. yo _____	a. repites
2. ellos _____	b. guio
3. tú _____	c. continúan
4. él _____	d. defiende
5. vosotras _____	e. distribuís
6. nosotros _____	f. pensamos

Exercise B

Use what you learned to fill in the gaps in the following verb charts.

1. *pensar*   to think

Person	Singular	Plural
1st	yo _____	nosotros pensamos
		nosotras _____
2nd	tú _____	vosotros _____
		vosotras _____
3rd	él _____	ellos _____
	ella piensa	ellas piensan
	usted piensa	ustedes _____

2. _____ to destroy

Person	Singular	Plural
1st	yo _____	nosotros destruimos
		nosotras destruimos
2nd	tú _____	vosotros _____
		vosotras destruís
3rd	él _____	ellos _____
	ella _____	ellas _____
	usted _____	ustedes _____

PART 2, Exercise A

Fill in the blanks with the correct form of the verb in parentheses.

1. Yo _____ *(dar) una manzana a la profesora.*

2. Tú _____ *(ser) muy simpático, Martín.*

3. ¿Vosotros _____ *(ir) al supermercado hoy?*

4. Yo _____ *(conocer) a la amiga de Pedro.*

5. Anita _____ *(tener) un perro y un gato.*

Exercise B

Select the right form of the verb. Circle the letter.

1. *Mi mamá* _____ *las llaves en la mesa.*
   - A. pone
   - B. pongo
   - C. ponemos

2. ¿Tú _____ el libro de español?

    A. tenemos
    B. tengo
    C. tienes

3. Vosotros _____ todas las mañanas.

    A. salís
    B. sale
    C. salgo

4. Ustedes _____ al gimnasio.

    A. voy
    B. van
    C. vamos

5. Yo _____ muy cansado.

    A. estás
    B. está
    C. estoy

Exercise C

Turn the present-tense verb into the present-progressive form. Rewrite the whole sentence.

1. Los señores leen el periódico (newspaper).

    _____

2. El bebé duerme.

    _____

3. Mi madre pide un café.

    _____

4. *Yo escribo una carta postal* (postcard) *a mi amiga.*

   _____

5. *Ellos le dan una cobija* (blanket).

   _____

6. *Nosotros comemos la cena* (dinner).

   _____

7. *Raúl y Juliana estudian para el examen.*

   _____

8. *La niña llora* (cries).

   _____

9. *La profesora habla.*

   _____

10. *Mi abuela cocina* (cooks).

    _____

LESSON 5

Lesson 6

Tricky Verbs

- *Saber* and *Conocer*
- *Tomar* and *Llevar*
- *Haber* and *Tener*

Direct and Indirect Object Pronouns

- Direct Objects
- Indirect Objects
- Direct Object Pronouns
- Indirect Object Pronouns
- Double Object Pronouns

Functional Language: Using *ir a* Expressions

Sample Test Questions

6

Tricky Verbs

There are a few Spanish verbs that stump students constantly because we commonly confuse their meanings. We've already discussed two of them, *ser* and *estar*. If you recall what you learned in Lesson 4:

ser (to be)	
Rule	**Example**
Can be used with adjectives that describe physical qualities	*El niño **es** simpático.*
Identifies people and things, such as occupations	*La señora **es** doctora.*
Expresses permanent conditions, such as nationalities	***Soy** española.*
Tells the time and date	*Hoy **es** jueves, y **son** las tres.*
Expresses possession	*La pluma **es** de Juanita.*

estar (to be)	
Rule	**Example**
Tells location	*El libro **está** en la biblioteca.*
Expresses conditions that are likely to change	***Estoy** muy cansado.*

One easy way to remember the difference between *ser* and *estar* is to memorize the expression **DON'T B LOCO**:

Ser: **D** (description) **O** (occupation) **N** (nationality) **T** (time/ weather/seasons) **B** (belonging, possessive adjectives)
Estar: **LO** (location) **CO** (condition).

Now let's learn about other verbs that change meaning.

SABER AND CONOCER

The verbs *saber* and *conocer* are similar to *ser* and *estar*. *Saber* and *conocer* both translate as "to know." However, they mean "to know" in two different senses.

▸ *Saber* means "to know something" or, when used with the infinitive, "to know how to do something."

    ¿**Sabes** mi dirección? *Do you know my address?*
    Sé hablar español. *I know how to speak Spanish.*

▸ *Conocer* means "to know someone or to be familiar with something."

    Conozco a Luis. *I know Luis.*
    No **conozco** la ciudad. *I'm not familiar with the city.*

> **Saber and Conocer** Saber and conocer *have irregular yo forms:*
> *yo sé, and yo conozco.*

TOMAR AND LLEVAR

Tomar and *llevar* both translate as "to take."

▸ *Tomar* means "to take something" or "to drink something."

    Tomo el autobús. *I take the bus.*
    Tomamos la llave. *We take the key.*
    ¿**Tomas** jugo? *Do you drink juice?*

▸ *Llevar* means "to take someone or something away."

    Llevo mi libro a la escuela. *I take my book to school.*
    Llevamos a mis padres al concierto. *We take my parents to the concert.*

HABER AND TENER

Haber and *tener* both translate as "to have."

▸ *Haber* is mostly used as *hay*. *Hay* is equivalent to "there is" or "there are." It does not have a subject.

    Hay un libro en la mesa. *There is a book on the table.*
    Hay tres estudiantes en el aula. *There are three students in the classroom.*

LESSON 6

> **PITFALL!** Hay *does not change to plural. It has no plural form.*
>
> **Hay** un libro en la biblioteca. *There is a book in the library.*
> **Hay** muchos libros en la biblioteca. *There are lots of books in the library.*

▸ *Tener* means "to have something."

> **Tengo** una bicicleta. *I have a bicycle.*
> **Tienen** dos hermanas. *They have two sisters.*

▸ As you learned in Lesson 5, *tener* is also used in idiomatic expressions.

> **Tengo** veinte años. *I'm twenty years old.*
> **Tengo** frío. *I'm cold.*
> **Tengo** hambre. *I'm hungry.*
> **Tengo** ganas de comer. *I feel like eating.*

Direct and Indirect Object Pronouns

At this point, we've covered all present-tense verbs. We're now ready to learn about direct and indirect object pronouns. However, let's review direct and indirect objects first.

DIRECT OBJECTS

What's a direct object? The direct object of a sentence is who or what is receiving the direct action of the verb. Take a look at the following sentences in English.

> subject   verb   direct object
> The woman feeds the **baby**.

> subject   verb   direct object
> María Clara eats **cereal**.

To identify the direct object of the first sentence, ask yourself: who does the woman feed? The answer is: the baby. To identify the direct object of the second sentence, ask yourself: what does María Clara eat? The answer is: cereal. These are the direct objects.

The Personal a

In Spanish, when the direct object of a verb is a person, always add an *a* after the verb. This is called the "personal *a*." The personal *a* signals that the person that follows is a direct object (and not the subject of the sentence). Take a look at these sentences.

Yo veo **a** Juan.   *I see Juan.*

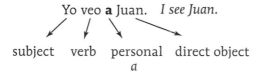

subject   verb   personal   direct object
a

In the following sentence, the personal *a* is not necessary. The direct object, *motocicleta*, is not a person.

Yo veo la motociecla.   *I see the motorcycle.*

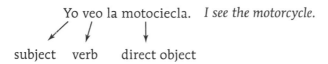

subject   verb   direct object

Make sure you contract the personal *a* and the definite article, *el*, to form *al*.

Invito **al** esposo de la vecina.   *I invite my neighbor's husband.*

INDIRECT OBJECTS

The **indirect object** of a sentence is whom or what is benefited (or harmed by) the action of the verb. Take a look at the following sentences, in English.

subject verb   indirect object
The boy gives a book to his **sister**.

subject   verb   indirect object
The woman puts powder on her **baby**.

To identify the indirect object of the first sentence, ask yourself: whom does the boy give the book to? The answer is: to his sister. To identify the indirect object of the second sentence, ask yourself: whom does the woman put powder on? The answer is: on her baby. These are the indirect objects.

When you're trying to identify the indirect object of a sentence in Spanish, always look for the prepositions *a* or *para*.

> **PITFALL!**   *Don't be misguided by the personal a, which has a different function than the preposition a.*

▸ When *a* precedes the indirect object, include *le* or *les* to the sentence. These are indirect object pronouns. We'll learn more about them later on in the lesson.

> indirect object
> **Le** doy una muñeca **a** mi hermana.   *I give a doll to my sister.*

> **PITFALL!**   *Include le only with a él and a ella, not with a ti or a mi or a nosotros, etc.*

▸ When *para* precedes the indirect object, do not include the indirect object pronoun.

> indirect object
> Compro una mesa **para** la cocina.   *I buy a table for the kitchen.*

> **Verbs Used with Indirect Objects** *Here are some verbs that are often used with indirect objects.*
>
> dar   *to give*
> decir   *to say*
> escribir   *to write*
> explicar   *to explain*
> ofrecer   *to offer*
> pedir   *to ask for*
> preguntar   *to ask*
> prestar   *to lend*
> regalar   *to give a gift*

DIRECT OBJECT PRONOUNS

Pronouns, as we've mentioned before, replace nouns. Direct object pronouns replace direct object nouns. Here they are:

For the singular:

Person		
1st	me	*me*
2nd	te	*you*
3rd	lo	*him, it* (masculine), *you* (formal)
	la	*her, it* (feminine), *you* (formal)

For the plural:

Person		
1st	nos	*us*
2nd	os	*you*
3rd	los	*them* (masculine), *you* (formal)
	las	*them* (feminine), *you* (formal)

Here are some examples:

Mauricio ve a **Federico**. Mauricio **lo** ve.   *Mauricio sees Federico. Mauricio sees him.*

Compro la **manzana**. **La** compro.   *I buy the apple. I buy it.*

Te veo.   *I see you.*
José **la** ve.   *José sees her.*
Los conozco bién.   *I know them well.*
Os entiendo.   *I understand you.*

The direct object pronoun comes before the verb, regardless of whether the sentence is affirmative or negative.

Marible tiene la **llave**. Maribel **la** tiene.   *Maribel has the key. Maribel has it.*
Maribel no tiene la **llave**. Maribel no **la** tiene.   *Maribel doesn't have the key. She doesn't have it.*

LESSON 6

INDIRECT OBJECT PRONOUNS

Indirect object pronouns replace indirect object nouns. Here they are:

For the singular:

Person		
1st	me	*to / for me*
2nd	te	*to / for you*
3rd	le	*to / for him, her, it, you* (formal)

For the plural:

Person		
1st	nos	*to / for us*
2nd	os	*to / for you*
3rd	les	*to / for them, you* (formal)

Here are some examples:

Yo **le** escribo una carta a **Susana**.   *I write a letter to Susanna.*

Tú **les** prestas dinera a **Martín y a Ramiro**.   *You lend money to Martín and Ramiro.*

If the indirect-object noun is known (for example, if you already know that the letter is for Susana and the money is for Martín and Ramiro), you can drop the indirect object noun. In this case, use only the indirect object pronoun. The preposition *a* is used when the indirect object is not understood.

Yo **le** escribo una carta.   *I write her a letter.*
Tú **les** prestas dinero.   *You lend them money.*

DOUBLE OBJECT PRONOUNS

Sometimes a verb has both a direct object pronoun and an indirect object pronoun. When this happens, the indirect object pronoun will always precede the direct object pronoun. This combination is called a double object pronoun.

Escribo una carta y **te la** mando. *I write a letter and send it to you.*

indirect object pronoun   direct object pronoun

The pronouns can go either before or after the verb. In the example above, the indirect object pronoun (*te*) appears after the verb (*escribo*). The direct object pronoun (*la*) appears before the verb (*mando*).

In some cases, both pronouns will go after the verb. They are attached to the verb. Don't forget to add an accent mark to preserve the verb's original stress.

Quiero **comprártelo**. *I want to buy it for you.*

Le and *les* change to *se* when followed by *lo, la, los,* or *las.*

Le vendo la mochila. *I sell him/her the backpack.*
Se la vendo. *I sell it to him/her.*

Les compro los lápices. *I buy them the pencils.*
Se los compro. *I buy them for them.*

Functional Language: Using *ir a* Expressions

The verb *ir* (to go) is irregular in the present tense.

ir (to go)		
Person	**Singular**	**Plural**
1st	yo **voy**	nosotros **vamos**
2nd	tú **vas**	vosotros **vais**
3rd	él **va**	ellos **van**
	ella **va**	ellas **van**
	usted **va**	ustedes **van**

▶ You will often see *ir* accompanied by the preposition *a* (to) and the definite article *el* (or *la*). When used with the masculine definite article, the construction is shortened to *ir al*, or "go to the . . ."

> ¿Adónde vas? **Voy al** gimnasio.   *Where are you going? I'm going to the gym.*

▶ *Vamos* is used to express "let's go."

> **Vamos** al supermercado.   *Let's go to the supermarket.*

▶ The construction *ir a* + infinitive is used to talk about or actions or events in the near future. The English equivalent is "to be going to" + infinitive.

> Mañana **voy a ir** al doctor.   *Tomorrow I'm going to go to the doctor.*

Sample Test Questions

PART 1, Exercise A

Write the correct verb from the parentheses in the blank.

1. _____ (Soy / Estoy) tu amiga.

2. _____ (Es / Está) alto y guapo.

3. _____ (Estáis / Sois) cansados.

4. _____ (Eres / Estás) estudiante.

5. _____ (Son / Están) americanas.

6. _____ Manú (es / está) mi gato.

7. _____ (Somos / Estamos) de Argentina.

8. _____ (Están / Son) felices hoy.

9. _____ Cantar (es / estar) vivir.

10. _____ ¿(Estás / Eres) aburrido con la lección?

Exercise B

Translate the following sentences into Spanish.

1. My boss (jefe) is rich.

   _____

2. Francisca is nine years old.

   _____

3. We drink milk (leche).

   _____

4. The boys know how to speak German (alemán).

   _____

5. There are two apples in the refrigerator (refrigeradora).

   _____

6. Do you take the bus to school?

   _____

Part 2, Exercise A

Change the direct object noun to a direct object pronoun. Make any other necessary changes.

1. Francisco tiene el pasaporte.

   _____

2. ¿Veis a Juan?

   _____

3. Leemos la lección.

   _____

4. El muchacho escribe el párrafo (paragraph).

   _____

5. Yo veo la película (movie).

   _____

Exercise B

Use the cues in parentheses to provide the indirect-object pronoun for the sentence. Write the pronoun in the space provided.

1. *Juan* _____ *escribe una carta.* (to Elena and Felipe)

2. *Maite* _____ *canta en español.* (to us)

3. *La profesora* _____ *enseña los verbos.* (to me)

4. *Nosotras* _____ *compramos un suéter.* (for her)

5. *Yo* _____ *doy una manzana.* (to you, informal)

Exercise C

Rewrite the following sentences. Change the underlined noun to a pronoun.

1. *Te mando <u>unos regalos</u>* (gifts).

   _____

2. *Le presto <u>mi pluma</u>.*

   _____

3. *Le enseño <u>la camisa (shirt) nueva</u>.*

   _____

4. *Nos compra <u>una bicicleta</u>.*

   _____

5. *¿Me traes* (bring) *<u>la bebida</u>* (drink)?

   _____

LESSON 6

Exercise D

Fill in the blank with the correct form of the verb. Write the verb in the space provided. Add the *a* + article.

ir   voy   vas   va   vamos   vais   van

1. *Mañana nosotros _____ gimnasio.*

2. *Yo _____ almacén* (store).

3. *Vosotros _____ biblioteca.*

4. *Jaime y José _____ piscina* (swimming pool).

5. *Rodrigo _____ museo.*

Lesson 7

Expressing Negation
- Indefinite and Negative Words
- Using Indefinite and Negative Words
- Indefinite and Negative Expressions
- *Pero* and *Sino*

The Preterite Tense
- Preterite Tense of Regular Verbs

Functional Language:
Expressing Likes and Dislikes

Sample Test Questions

7

Expressing Negation

As in English, the word *no* is used to express negation or refusal in Spanish.

> ¿Quieres tu abrigo?   *Do you want your coat?*
> **No,** gracias.   *No, thank you.*

In Spanish the word *no* always precedes the verb it negates. Take a look at these examples.

> Sara **no** tiene computadora.   *Sara does not have a computer.*
> **No** puedo comer.   *I can't eat.*

INDEFINITE AND NEGATIVE WORDS

▶ Indefinite words refer to nonspecific people and things.

> **Someone** left the lights on.
> Do you want **something** from the store?

▶ Negative words, on the other hand, deny the existence of people and things.

> **No one** is here today.
> There is **nothing** to eat in the fridge.

Here is a list of the most common indefinite words in Spanish, and the negatives to which they correspond. Try to learn them together.

Negative		Indefinite	
nada	*nothing, not anything*	algo	*something*
nadie	*no one, not anyone, nobody*	alguien	*someone, anyone*
nadie	*nobody, no one, not anything*	cualquiera	*anybody, any*
ninguno, ninguna,	*no, no one, none, neither*	alguno, alguna	*some, someone, any*
ninguno	*nobody, no one, none, not any*	algunos, algunas, unos	*some, several, any*

nunca, jamás	*never*	alguna vez	*ever*
		siempre	*always*
tampoco	*neither, not either*	también	*also, too*

Note: *Ninguno(-a)* is only used in the singular form.

USING INDEFINITE AND NEGATIVE WORDS

In Spanish, indefinite words are generally easy to use, as they often parallel English usage. Negative words, however, are a little trickier, as the rules contradict English grammar principles. You'll notice that double (and multiple) negatives are common in Spanish—in fact, sometimes you *must* use a double negative.

Here are the rules:

▸ If *no* or another negative word comes before the verb, all words that follow must be negative.

> **No** quiero **nada**.   *I don't want anything* (literally, "I don't want nothing")
> **No** canta **ninguno** de mis hermanos.   *None of my siblings sing.*

▸ If a negative word comes before the verb, don't use the word *no*.

> **Nunca** como ensalada.   *I never eat salad.*

Here are some more rules to follow when using indefinite and negative words.

Alguien and Nadie

▸ *Alguien* and *nadie* refer to people and are always in the singular. When *alguien* or *nadie* is the direct object of a verb, you must use the word *a* before it. This, as we learned in Lesson 6, is the "personal *a*."

Remember, to identify the direct object of a verb, ask yourself: who or what is receiving the direct action of the verb? You can work it out by first naming the subject and then figuring out which noun/pronoun is the subject and which is the direct object.

LESSON 7

verb   direct object
¿Conoces **a alguien** aquí?   *Do you know anyone here?*

verb   direct object
No conozco **a nadie** aquí.   *I don't know anyone here.*

▶ When *alguien* or *nadie* is the subject of the sentence, it does not require *a*.

Alguien te llama.   *Someone is calling you.*
Nadie está en casa.   *No one's home.*

Alguno and Ninguno

▶ *Alguno* and *ninguno* refer to objects or people. When *alguno* and *ninguno* come in front of a masculine, singular noun, they are shortened to *algún* and *ningún*.

¿Hay **algún** libro aquí?   *Are there any books here?*
No hay **ningún** libro aquí.   *There are no books here.*

▶ Again, use the personal *a* when *alguno* or *ninguno* is the direct object of a verb and refers to a person.

verb   direct object
¿Conoces **a algún** profesor?   *Do you know any teachers?*

verb   direct object
No conozco **a ningún** profesor.   *I don't know any teachers.*

verb   direct object
Veo **a algunas** niñas en el parque.   *I see some girls at the park.*

▶ As you can see from the above example, *alguno* can be plural (*algunos*).

También and Tampoco

▶ *También* expresses agreement with an affirmative statement.

Quiero ir.   *I want to go.* ⟶ Yo quiero ir **también**.   *I want to go too.*

▸ *Tampoco* expresses agreement with a negative statement.

No quiero ir. *I don't want to go.* ⟶ Yo no quiero ir **tampoco**. *I don't want to go either.*

Note that in the second example, the word *no* forces us to use the negative *tampoco*, which is translated as "not either."

INDEFINITE AND NEGATIVE EXPRESSIONS

Here are some key expressions with indefinite and negative words.

Negative Expressions		Indefinite Expressions	
en ninguna parte	*nowhere*	en alguna parte	*somewhere*
de ninguna manera	*in no way*	de alguna manera	*somehow*
ni siquiera	*not even*	alguna vez	*ever*
ya no	*no longer*	algunas veces	*sometimes*
todavía no	*not yet*		

El lápiz tiene que estar en **alguna parte**. *The pencil has to be somewhere.*
Ya no sé hablar inglés. *I don't know how to speak English anymore.*

PERO AND SINO

Pero and *sino* often accompany negative and affirmative words. Both mean "but." However, they are used differently.

▸ *Pero* means "but nevertheless."

No soy norteamericano, **pero** hablo inglés. *I'm not American, but nevertheless, I speak English.*

▸ *Sino*, on the other hand, means "but rather."

Los libros no son viejos **sino** nuevos. *The books are not old but, rather, new.*

Pero links two complete sentences—there has to be a conjugated verb on each "side" of the *pero*. *Sino* has a sentence on one side and a word or phrase on the other.

LESSON 7

The Preterite Tense

Let's shift gears for a moment and return to verbs for a discussion of the past tense.

Spanish uses two simple tenses to speak about the past: the preterite and the imperfect.

The preterite tense is used to express actions or states completed in the past.

Ayer **comí** dos caramelos.   *Yesterday I ate two candies.*

You'll learn more about the uses of the preterite tense in Lesson 10.

PRETERITE TENSE OF REGULAR VERBS

In Lesson 3 we explained that all regular Spanish verbs have a stem that stays the same when the verb is conjugated. This holds true for the preterite tense, too. Let's look at stems again.

cantar   **com**er   **escrib**ir

To form the preterite tense of a regular verb, first drop the infinitive ending: *-ar, -er, -ir.*

Then add the following endings to the stem.

-ar Verbs

For singular *-ar* verbs, add *-é, -aste,* and *-ó.*

cantar (to sing)		
Person	**Singular**	
1st	yo canté	*I sang*
2nd	tú cantaste	*you sang*
3rd	él cantó	*he sang*
	ella cantó	*she sang*
	usted cantó	*you sang* (formal)

For plural -ar verbs, add -amos, -asteis, and -aron.

Person	Plural	
1st	nosotros cantamos	*we sang* (masculine)
	nosotras cantamos	*we sang* (feminine)
2nd	vosotros cantasteis	*you sang* (plural, masculine)
	vosotras cantasteis	*you sang* (plural, feminine)
3rd	ellos cantaron	*they sang* (masculine)
	ellas cantaron	*they sang* (feminine)
	ustedes cantaron	*you sang* (plural, formal)

Sequence Words *Use sequence words to talk about things you did or have done in the past. Sequence words put these events in order, and you'll need to know them when studying the past tense.*

primero . . .   *first . . .*
luego . . .   *then . . .*
después . . .   *afterwards . . .*
finalmente . . .   *finally . . .*
por fin . . .   *finally . . .*

-er and -ir Verbs

For singular -er and -ir verbs, add -í, -iste, and -ió.

comer (to eat)		
Person	Singular	
1st	yo comí	*I ate*
2nd	tú comiste	*you ate*
3rd	él comió	*he ate*
	ella comió	*she ate*
	usted comió	*you ate* (formal)

escribir (to write)		
Person	**Singular**	
1st	yo escribí	*I wrote*
2nd	tú escribiste	*you wrote*
3rd	él escribió	*he wrote*
	ella escribió	*she wrote*
	usted escribió	*you wrote* (formal)

For plural *-er* and *-ir* verbs, add *-imos*, *-isteis*, and *-ieron*.

Person	**Plural**	
1st	nosotros comimos	*we ate* (masculine)
	nosotras comimos	*we ate* (feminine)
2nd	vosotros comisteis	*you ate* (plural, masculine)
	vosotras comisteis	*you ate* (plural, feminine)
3rd	ellos comieron	*they ate* (masculine)
	ellas comieron	*they ate* (feminine)
	ustedes comieron	*you ate* (plural, formal)

Person	**Plural**	
1st	nosotros escribimos	*we wrote* (masculine)
	nosotras escribimos	*we wrote* (feminine)
2nd	vosotros escribisteis	*you wrote* (plural, masculine)
	vosotras escribisteis	*you wrote* (plural, feminine)
3rd	ellos escribieron	*they wrote* (masculine)
	ellas escribieron	*they wrote* (feminine)
	ustedes escribieron	*you wrote* (plural, formal)

We will learn more about the preterite tense in Lesson 8.

Functional Language: Expressing Likes and Dislikes

To say you like something, use the verb *gustar*. The verb *gustar* literally means "to be pleasing," although we translate it as "to like."

Me **gusta** la clase de inglés.   *English class is pleasing to me. =*
    I like English class.
¿**No** te **gustó** la película?   *The movie wasn't pleasing to you? =*
    You didn't like the movie?

Here is what you need to know about *gustar*:

▶ The verb must agree with the subject of the sentence. For example, when the subject of the sentence is plural, use *gustan*.

plural verb   plural subject
Nos gustan los **dulces**.   *Sweets please us. / We like sweets.*

▶ *Gustar* is always used with an indirect object pronoun. Someone or something needs to be pleasing to someone else.

Me gusta el café.   *Coffee is pleasing to me. / I like coffee.*
Le gusta la comida china.   *Chinese food is pleasing to him/her. / He/she likes Chinese food.*

PITFALL!	In Me gusta el café, me is not the subject. Don't say yo me gusta el café either. The thing liked is the subject, not the person who likes.

Indirect Object Pronouns Here are the indirect object pronouns.

Person	Singular	Plural
1st	me	nos
2nd	te	os
3rd	le	les

▶ *Gustar* can be followed by an infinitive. An infinitive (or group of infinitives) is viewed as a singular subject.

Me gusta **comer** a las ocho de la mañana.   *I like to eat at eight in the morning.*
Me gusta **correr**, **saltar**, y **brincar**.   *I like to run, jump, and hop.*

LESSON 7

▶ The phrase *a* + noun/pronoun is often used to clarify or emphasize.

To clarify:

A mí me gusta leer, pero **a ti** te gusta cantar.   *I like to read, but you like to sing.*

To emphasize:

A Teodoro le gusta la música rock.   *Teodoro likes rock music.*

> **PITFALL!**   *In sentences like* A Teodoro le gusta la música rock, *make sure you don't leave out the* a *and say* Teodoro le gusta la música rock.

▶ If you'd like to say "would like to do" or "would not like to do" in Spanish, you can use the form *gustaría* + infinitive. This is a form that you will learn later in your Spanish studies.

Me **gustaría** ir a Egipto.   *I'd like to go to Egypt.*
No nos **gustaría** comer pollo.   *We wouldn't like to eat chicken.*

> **Other Verbs Like Gustar** *There are other verbs that function as* gustar *does. Here they are:*
>
> encantar   *to like very much, to adore*
> faltar   *to be lacking*
> fascinar   *to fascinate*
> importar   *to matter*
> interesar   *to be interesting to*
> molestar   *to bother*

Sample Test Questions

Rewrite the following affirmative sentences as negative sentences. There may be more than one answer. Remember the rules for double negatives.

1. *Algunos de mis amigos viven allí.*

   _____

2. *Necesitamos algo.* (necesitar = to need)

   _____

3. *Siempre estudio con alguien.*

   _____

4. *¿Queréis ir a la fiesta* (party)*?*

   _____

5. *Hay algo en la refrigeradora.*

   _____

6. *Siempre coméis desayuno* (breakfast)*.*

   _____

7. *Conozco a algún niño americano.*

   _____

8. *Siempre voy al gimnasio* (gym)*.*

   _____

LESSON 7

9. Los alumnos tienen una computadora.

_____

10. Amo a alguien. (amar = to love)

_____

Exercise B

Fill in the blank with the appropriate word: *también*, *tampoco*, *sino*, or *pero*.

1. Victoria no quiere café, ni yo _____.

2. No soy fea (ugly), _____ bonita (pretty).

3. Ellos necesitan un suéter. Ellas _____ necesitan un suéter.

4. Juan Pablo no come carne, _____ sí come pescado (fish).

5. Soy ecuatoriana. Marta _____ es ecuatoriana.

6. El profesor no es bueno, _____ malo.

7. La televisión es vieja _____ todavía funciona. (*funcionar* = to work, function properly)

8. El gato no es vegetariano. El perro _____ es vegetariano.

9. Mi abuelo (grandfather) toma medicina. Mi abuela _____ toma medicina.

10. El programa no es interesante, _____ aburrido (boring).

PART 2, Exercise A

Fill in the blanks with the preterite form of the verb in parentheses.

1. *Mi tía Carlota* _____ *(vender) su carro.*

2. *Ayer yo* _____ *(comer) una ensalada verde* (green salad).

3. *¿Vosotros* _____ *(correr) en el parque?*

4. *Manuel, ¿* _____ *(cerrar) la ventana* (window)?

5. *La niña* _____ *(llegar) tarde a la escuela.*

6. *Mi equipo* (team) _____ *(ganar) el campeonato* (championship).

7. *Vosotros* _____ *(escribir) un libro.*

8. *Francisca* _____ *(estudiar) el la biblioteca.*

9. *Mi hermana* _____ *(vivir) en España el año pasado* (last year).

10. *Yo no* _____ *(comprender =* understand) *la pregunta.*

Exercise B

Conjugate the following verbs in the preterite tense.

1. *Yo* _____ *(compartir =* share).

2. *Nosotros* _____ *(comer).*

3. *Vosotras* _____ *(vivir).*

4. *Tú* _____ *(comprar).*

5. *Ellos* _____ *(vender).*

6. *Él* _____ *(escribir).*

7. Yo _____ (celebrar).

8. Ella _____ (preparar).

9. Yo _____ (recibir).

10. Usted _____ (enseñar).

Exercise C

Fill in the blank with the correct form of *gustar* in the present tense and the correct pronoun. Write your answer in the space provided.

1. A mí no _____ viajar.

2. A Magdalena _____ el pescado frito (fried fish).

3. A nosotros _____ leer revistas (magazines).

4. A tus hermanos _____ correr en el parque.

5. Al niño no _____ los perros.

6. A vosotros no _____ los bichos (bugs).

7. A ti _____ comer hamburguesas.

8. A ella no _____ leer.

9. A mis padres _____ cocinar cada (every) noche.

10. A nosotros _____ la televisión.

Lesson 8

The Preterite Tense of Other Verbs
- The Preterite Tense of Stem-Changing Verbs
- Verbs with Spelling Changes
- Irregular Verbs

Verbs That Change Meaning in the Preterite Tense

Reflexive Verbs

Reflexive Pronouns
- Stem-Changing Reflexive Verbs

Functional Language: Expressing Physical and Mental Changes

Sample Test Questions

8

The Preterite Tense of Other Verbs

In Lesson 7, we learned how to conjugate the preterite tense of regular *-ar*, *-er*, and *-ir* verbs. Now let's learn how to conjugate verbs that are not regular.

THE PRETERITE TENSE OF STEM-CHANGING VERBS

In Lesson 5, we introduced stem-changing verbs. As you remember, when stem-changing verbs are conjugated in the present tense, they undergo spelling changes that follow regular patterns. Luckily, for *-ar* and *-er* verbs this does not happen in the preterite.

▶ cerrar   *to close*

> present: Ana **cierra** la puerta.   *Ana closes the door.*
> preterite: Ana **cerró** la puerta.   *Ana closed the door.*

▶ volver   *to come back*

> present: Simón **vuelve** a las cinco.   *Simón comes back at five o'clock.*
> preterite: Simón **volvió** a las cinco.   *Simón came back at five o'clock.*

Note how these verbs had spelling changes in their stems in the present but not in the preterite.

However, for verbs that end in *-ir* and have a stem change in the present tense, there is a stem change in the preterite tense as well.

e → i

Verbs that have a stem change from *e* to *ie* in the present tense have a stem change in the third-person singular and the third-person plural of the preterite tense. The change is from *e* to *i*.

preferir (to prefer)		
Person	**Singular**	
1st	yo preferí	*I preferred*
2nd	tú preferiste	*you preferred*
3rd	él prefirió	*he preferred*
	ella prefirió	*she preferred*
	usted prefirió	*you preferred* (formal)
Person	**Plural**	
1st	nosotros preferimos	*we preferred* (masculine)
	nosotras preferimos	*we preferred* (feminine)
2nd	vosotros preferisteis	*you preferred* (plural, masculine)
	vosotras preferisteis	*you preferred* (plural, feminine)
3rd	ellos prefirieron	*they preferred* (masculine)
	ellas prefirieron	*they preferred* (feminine)
	ustedes prefirieron	*you preferred* (plural, formal)

There is another case in which a stem change from *e* to *i* occurs. Verbs that have a stem change from *e* to *i* in the present tense have a stem change in the third-person singular and the third-person plural of the preterite tense.

vestir (to dress)		
Person	**Singular**	
1st	yo vestí	*I dressed*
2nd	tú vestiste	*you dressed*
3rd	él vistió	*he dressed*
	ella vistió	*she dressed*
	usted vistió	*you dressed* (formal)
Person	**Plural**	
1st	nosotros vestimos	*we dressed* (masculine)
	nosotras vestimos	*we dressed* (feminine)
2nd	vosotros vestisteis	*you dressed* (plural, masculine)
	vosotras vestisteis	*you dressed* (plural, feminine)
3rd	ellos vistieron	*they dressed* (masculine)
	ellas vistieron	*they dressed* (feminine)
	ustedes vistieron	*you dressed* (plural, formal)

o → u

Similarly, verbs that have a stem change from *o* to *ue* in the present tense have a stem change in the third-person singular and the third-person plural of the preterite tense. The change is from *o* to *u*.

dormir (to sleep)		
Person	**Singular**	
1st	yo dormí	*I slept*
2nd	tú dormiste	*you slept*
3rd	él d**u**rmió	*he slept*
	ella d**u**rmió	*she slept*
	usted d**u**rmió	*you slept* (formal)
Person	**Plural**	
1st	nosotros dormimos	*we slept* (masculine)
	nosotras dormimos	*we slept* (feminine)
2nd	vosotros dormisteis	*you slept* (plural, masculine)
	vosotras dormisteis	*you slept* (plural, feminine)
3rd	ellos d**u**rmieron	*they slept* (masculine)
	ellas d**u**rmieron	*they slept* (feminine)
	ustedes d**u**rmieron	*you slept* (plural, formal)

VERBS WITH SPELLING CHANGES

There are other verbs that have slight spelling changes in the preterite form. They are listed below.

-car, -gar, -zar

Verbs that end in *-car*, *-gar*, and *-zar* have changes in the first-person singular of the preterite tense. These changes aren't arbitrary. As you will see, the changes preserve the sound of the consonant.

▸ Verbs that end in *-car* change *c* to *qu*.

buscar (to look for)		
Person	**Singular**	
1st	yo bus**qu**é	*I looked for*
2nd	tú buscaste	*you looked for*
3rd	él buscó	*he looked for*
	ella buscó	*she looked for*
	usted buscó	*you looked for* (formal)

▸ Verbs that end in *-gar* change *g* to *gu*.

llegar (to arrive)		
Person	**Singular**	
1st	yo lle**gu**é	*I arrived*
2nd	tú llegaste	*you arrived*
3rd	él llegó	*he arrived*
	ella llegó	*she arrived*
	usted llegó	*you arrived* (formal)

▸ Verbs that end in *-zar* change *z* to *c*.

empezar (to start)		
Person	**Singular**	
1st	yo empe**c**é	*I started*
2nd	tú empezaste	*you started*
3rd	él empezó	*he started*
	ella empezó	*she started*
	usted empezó	*you started* (formal)

-aer, -eer, -uir, oír

Verbs that end in *-aer*, *-eer*, and *-uir* and the verb *oír* (to hear) change *i* to *y* in the third-person singular and the third-person plural.

caer (to fall)		
Person	**Singular**	
1st	yo caí	*I fell*
2nd	tú caíste	*you fell*
3rd	él cayó	*he fell*
	ella cayó	*she fell*
	usted cayó	*you fell* (formal)
Person	**Plural**	
1st	nosotros caímos	*we fell* (masculine)
	nosotras caímos	*we fell* (feminine)
2nd	vosotros caísteis	*you fell* (plural, masculine)
	vosotras caísteis	*you fell* (plural, feminine)
3rd	ellos cayeron	*they fell* (masculine)
	ellas cayeron	*they fell* (feminine)
	ustedes cayeron	*you fell* (plural, formal)

oír (to hear)		
Person	**Singular**	
1st	yo oí	*I heard*
2nd	tú oíste	*you heard*
3rd	él oyó	*he heard*
	ella oyó	*she heard*
	usted oyó	*you heard* (formal)
Person	**Plural**	
1st	nosotros oímos	*we heard* (masculine)
	nosotras oímos	*we heard* (feminine)
2nd	vosotros oísteis	*you heard* (plural, masculine)
	vosotras oísteis	*you heard* (plural, feminine)
3rd	ellos oyeron	*they heard* (masculine)
	ellas oyeron	*they heard* (feminine)
	ustedes oyeron	*you heard* (plural, formal)

IRREGULAR VERBS

Just as there are irregular verbs in the present tense, there are irregular verbs in the preterite tense. Irregular verbs, as we have learned, do not take the endings that -*ar*, -*er*, and -*ir* verbs take when conjugated.

u-Stem, i-Stem, j-Stem

Some Spanish verbs have irregular stems in the preterite tense. However, they do share a common set of endings: *-e, -iste, -o, -imos, -isteis, -ieron*.

Here are some examples of verbs with irregular stems. Take a look at the verb charts at the end of the book for their complete conjugations.

u-stem		*i*-stem		*j*-stem	
andar	(anduv-)	hacer	(hic-)	conducir	(conduj-)
estar	(estuv-)	querer	(quis-)	decir	(dij-)
tener	(tuv-)	venir	(vin-)	producir	(produj-)
poder	(pud-)			traer	(traj-)
poner	(pus-)				
saber	(sup-)				

> **PITFALL!** *J-stem verbs have a common irregular j-stem, but a different set of endings from those you have just learned: -e, -iste, -o, imos, -isteis, -eron.*

Other Irregulars

▶ The verbs *dar* and *ver* take regular *-er* endings, but without the accent marks.

dar (to give)		
Person	**Singular**	
1st	yo di	*I gave*
2nd	tú diste	*you gave*
3rd	él dio	*he gave*
	ella dio	*she gave*
	usted dio	*you gave* (formal)
Person	**Plural**	
1st	nosotros dimos	*we gave* (masculine)
	nosotras dimos	*we gave* (feminine)
2nd	vosotros disteis	*you gave* (plural, masculine)
	vosotras disteis	*you gave* (plural, feminine)
3rd	ellos dieron	*they gave* (masculine)
	ellas dieron	*they gave* (feminine)
	ustedes dieron	*you gave* (plural, formal)

ver (to see)		
Person	**Singular**	
1st	yo vi	*I saw*
2nd	tú viste	*you saw*
3rd	él vio	*he saw*
	ella vio	*she saw*
	usted vio	*you saw* (formal)
Person	**Plural**	
1st	nosotros vimos	*we saw* (masculine)
	nosotras vimos	*we saw* (feminine)
2nd	vosotros visteis	*you saw* (plural, masculine)
	vosotras visteis	*you saw* (plural, feminine)
3rd	ellos vieron	*they saw* (masculine)
	ellas vieron	*they saw* (feminine)
	ustedes vieron	*you saw* (plural, formal)

▸ The verbs *ir* and *ser* are identical in the preterite.

ir (to go) / ser (to be)		
Person	**Singular**	
1st	yo fui	*I went / was*
2nd	tú fuiste	*you went / were*
3rd	él fue	*he went / was*
	ella fue	*she went / was*
	usted fue	*you went / was* (formal)
Person	**Plural**	
1st	nosotros fuimos	*we went / were* (masculine)
	nosotras fuimos	*we went / were* (feminine)
2nd	vosotros fuisteis	*you went / were* (plural, masculine)
	vosotras fuisteis	*you went / were* (plural, feminine)
3rd	ellos fueron	*they went / were* (masculine)
	ellas fueron	*they went / were* (feminine)
	ustedes fueron	*you went / were* (plural, formal)

LESSON 8

PITFALL! *Irregular preterites have no written accent marks.*

Verbs That Change Meaning in the Preterite Tense

Some verbs, when used in the preterite, have special meanings.

	Present	**Preterite**
poder	to be able	to succeed

¿Puedes ayudarme, por favor?   *Can you help me, please?*
Por fin pudiste alcanzar tu meta.   *You finally succeeded in reaching your goal.*

no poder	not to be able	not to succeed, to fail

No puedo ir al cine.   *I cannot go to the movies.*
No pude terminar la tarea.   *I was not able to finish my homework.*

conocer	to know	to meet (for the first time)

Yo lo conozco.   *I know him.*
Yo lo conocí en la fiesta.   *I met him at the party.*

querer	to want	to try, to attempt

La niña quiere su muñeca.   *The girl wants her doll.*
Mi padre quiso abrir la ventana.   *My dad tried to open the window.*

no querer	not to want	to refuse

No queremos estudiar.   *We don't want to study.*
No quisimos ir a la biblioteca.   *We refused to go to the library.*

saber	to know	to find out

Sé hablar francés.   *I know how to speak French.*
Supe eso anoche.   *I found out last night.*

Reflexive Verbs

At this point, we've gone over direct and indirect objects a couple of times. Remember that the direct object of a sentence is who or what is receiving the direct action of the verb, while the indirect object of a sentence is whom or what is benefited by (or harmed by) the action of the verb.

When either the direct object or the indirect object of a sentence is the same person or thing as the subject, the sentence is reflexive. In other words, the action of the verb is "reflected" back to the subject.

Reflexive verbs are used to indicate that the subject is doing something to or for himself or herself.

A reflexive verb is a verb in the infinitive with an -se ending.

> lavarse   *to wash oneself*
> levantarse   *to get up*

Here are some more reflexive verbs.

> acostarse   *to go to bed*
> bañarse   *to bathe*
> cepillarse   *to brush*
> despedirse de   *to say goodbye to*
> despertarse   *to wake up*
> dormirse   *to go to sleep*
> llamarse   *to be called/named*
> peinarse   *to comb one's hair*
> ponerse   *to put on*
> preocuparse   *to worry about*
> probarse   *to try on*
> quedarse   *to stay*
> quitarse   *to take off*
> sentarse   *to sit down*
> sentirse   *to feel*
> vestirse   *to get dressed*

Reflexive Pronouns

Take a look at the following sentence. Do you see the pronoun? Reflexive verbs always use reflexive pronouns.

subject   reflexive verb
Yo <u>me</u> **lavo**.   *I wash myself.*

↓

reflexive pronoun

Here are the reflexive pronouns.

For the singular:

Person		
1st	me	*myself*
2nd	te	*yourself*
3rd	se	*herself*
		himself
		itself
		yourself (formal)

For the plural:

Person		
1st	nos	*ourselves*
2nd	os	*yourselves*
3rd	se	*themselves*
		yourselves (formal)

Reflexive pronouns follow the same rules for placement as object pronouns. They usually appear before the conjugated verb.

Examples:

Ellos **se visten**.   *They dress themselves.*
Yo **me cepillo** los dientes.   *I brush my teeth.*

In Spanish, unlike English, possessive adjectives (*mi, tu, su*, etc.) are not used with parts of the body.

María se lava **la** cara.   *María washes her face.*

STEM-CHANGING REFLEXIVE VERBS

Don't forget that some reflexive verbs have stem changes too.

> acostarse   (o → ue)
> La niña se ac**ue**sta a las siete.   *The girl goes to bed at seven.*

> despedirse de   (e → i)
> Me desp**i**do de mi abuela.   *I say goodbye to my grandmother.*

> dormirse   (o → ue)
> Siempre me d**ue**rmo en el bus.   *I always fall asleep on the bus.*

> probarse   (o → ue)
> La muchacha se pr**ue**ba el sombrero.   *The girl tries on the hat.*

> sentarse   (e → ie)
> La mujer se s**ie**nta en la banca.   *The woman sits on the bench.*

> sentirse   (e → ie)
> ¿Te s**ie**ntes bien?   *Do you feel all right?*

> vestirse   (e → i)
> El cura se v**i**ste de negro.   *The priest wears black.*

Idiomatic Expressions with Reflexive Verbs

Some reflexive verbs have an idiomatic meaning. These verbs don't necessarily indicate an action done to or for oneself. However, their constructions are reflexive.

> acordarse de   *to remember*
> arrepentirse de   *to repent*
> atreverse a   *to dare*
> burlarse de   *to make fun of*
> irse   *to go away*
> olvidarse de   *to forget*
> parecerse a   *to look like*
> quejarse   *to complain*
> reírse   *to laugh at*
> tratarse de   *to be about*

Examples:

> ¿**Te acuerdas** de Daniel?   *Do you remember Daniel?*
> Los niños **se burlan** de la niña.   *The boys make fun of the girl.*

Functional Language: Expressing Physical and Mental Changes

Spanish also uses reflexive verbs to express physical or mental changes. In English, we would express such changes by "to get" or "to become." Take a look at the following examples.

asustarse   *to get scared*
cansarse   *to get tired*
casarse   *to get married*
desmayarse   *to faint*
enfadarse   *to get angry*
enojarse   *to get angry*
resfriarse   *to catch a cold*

Examples:

> No puedo ver sangre, porque **me desmayo**.   *I can't see blood, because I faint.*
> Rosa **se asusta** al ver un ratón.   *Rosa gets scared when she sees a mouse.*

Sample Test Questions

Fill in the blank with the correct preterite-tense form of the verb in parentheses.

1. Ayer Felipe _____ en la casa de sus tíos. (dormir)

2. Raquel _____ comer comida japonesa. (preferir)

3. Tú y yo _____ a la fiesta tarde. (llegar)

4. Doña Camila _____ dos panes al cliente. (dar)

5. Yo le _____ que no puedo ir a la reunión. (decir)

Exercise B

Translate the following sentences into Spanish. Use the following words: *conocer*, *saber*, *querer*, and *poder*.

1. We met the new professor yesterday.

   _____

2. Last night (anoche) I succeeded in finishing my homework.

   _____

3. Nancy finally learned the truth.

   _____

4. They tried to buy a new car, but they didn't have enough (suficiente) money.

   _____

   _____

PART 2, Exercise A

Now translate these sentences into Spanish.

1. *I bathe myself every day.*

   _____

2. *Zoila tries on the shoes.*

   _____

3. *My father gets up at six in the morning.*

   _____

4. *The lady takes off her glasses* (lentes).

   _____

5. *Do you wash your face in the morning?*

   _____

6. *My best friend gets mad.*

   _____

7. *Federico falls asleep at eleven o'clock.*

   _____

8. *The teacher sits on the desk* (escritorio).

   _____

LESSON 8

Exercise B

Use what you learned to fill in the gaps in these reflexive verb charts.

1. cansarse

Person	Singular	Plural
1st	yo _____	nosotros _____
		nosotras _____
2nd	tú _____	vosotros _____
		vosotras _____
3rd	él _____	ellos _____
	ella _____	ellas _____
	usted _____	ustedes _____

2. enojarse

Person	Singular	Plural
1st	yo _____	nosotros _____
		nosotras _____
2nd	tú _____	vosotros _____
		vosotras _____
3rd	él _____	ellos _____
	ella _____	ellas _____
	usted _____	ustedes _____

3. *irse*

Person	Singular	Plural
1st	yo _____	nosotros _____
		nosotras _____
2nd	tú _____	vosotros _____
		vosotras _____
3rd	él _____	ellos _____
	ella _____	ellas _____
	usted _____	ustedes _____

4. *reírse*

Person	Singular	Plural
1st	yo _____	nosotros _____
		nosotras _____
2nd	tú _____	vosotros _____
		vosotras _____
3rd	él _____	ellos _____
	ella _____	ellas _____
	usted _____	ustedes _____

LESSON 8

Lesson 9

Comparisons
- Comparisons of Equality
- Comparisons of Inequality

Superlatives
- Irregular Superlatives
- Absolute Superlatives

Prepositions
- Pronouns After Prepositions
- Compound Prepositions
- Individual Prepositions
- The Prepositions *para* and *por*
- Verbs Without Prepositions

Functional Language: Using *¿qué?* and *¿cuál?*
- *¿Qué?*
- *¿Cuál?*

Sample Test Questions

9

Comparisons

Both Spanish and English use comparisons to compare people or things with one another. There are three kinds of comparisons: *equal to*, *greater than*, and *less than*.

COMPARISONS OF EQUALITY

When you are comparing two or more items that are equal, use the following constructions.

▶ With adjectives and adverbs: *tan* + adjective + *como* or *tan* + adverb + *como*

                               adjective

La comida en la universidad es **tan** buena **como** en casa.   *The food at the university is as good as it is at home.*

                     adverb

María habla **tan** bien **como** tú.   *María speaks as well as you do.*

▶ With singular nouns: *tanto* + masculine singular noun + *como* or *tanta* + feminine singular noun + *como*

                   masc. sing. noun

Sandra tiene **tanto** dinero **como** Ana.   *Sandra has as much money as Ana does.*

                fem. sing. noun

Tú comes **tanta** comida **como** mi padre.   *You eat as much food as my father does.*

▶ With plural nouns: *tantos* + masculine plural noun + *como* or *tantas* + feminine plural noun + *como*

                    masc. pl. noun

Ustedes prueban **tantos** platos **como** nosotros.   *You try as many dishes as we do.*

                fem. pl. noun

Yo tengo **tantas** amigas **como** mi hermana.   *I have as many friends as my sister does.*

▶ With verbs: verb + *tanto como*

> verb
> Yo duermo **tanto como** mi tía.   *I sleep as much as my aunt.*

COMPARISONS OF INEQUALITY

When you are comparing two or more items and one is greater than the other, use the following constructions.

▶ With adjectives and adverbs: *más* + adjective + *que* or *más* + adverb + *que*

> adjective
> El elefante es **más** grande **que** el caballo.   *The elephant is bigger then the horse.*

> adverb
> Me acuesto **más** tarde **que** tú.   *I go to bed later than you do.*

▶ With nouns: *más* + noun + *que*

> noun
> Elisa tiene **más** discos compactos **que** Zoila.   *Elisa has more compact discs than Zoila does.*

▶ With verbs: verb + *más que*

> verb
> Mi abuelo duerme **más que** mi abuela.   *My grandfather sleeps more than my grandmother does.*

When you are comparing two or more items and one is less than the other, use the following constructions.

▶ With adjectives and adverbs: *menos* + adjective + *que* and *menos* + adverb + *que*

LESSON 9

adjective
La biología es **menos** interesante **que** la química.   *Biology is less interesting than chemistry.*

adverb
Mi hermano corre **menos** rápido **que** Alfred.   *My brother runs less quickly than Alfred does.*

▶ With nouns: *menos* + noun + *que*

noun
Yo compro **menos** camisas **que** Roberto.   *I buy fewer shirts than Roberto does.*

▶ With verbs: verb + *menos que*

verb
El bébé de Marta llora **menos que** el bébé de Adelia.
Marta's baby cries less than Adelia's baby does.

Más de When you are comparing numbers of items, use the expressions más de and menos de. In other words, replace the que with de.

Tengo **más de** veinte libros.   *I have more than twenty books.*
Hay **menos de** diez estudiantes en la clase.   *There are fewer than ten students in the class.*

Irregular Comparison Forms

Some adjectives and adverbs have irregular comparison forms. Do not use *más* and *menos* with these words. Take a look at the following charts.

Adjective		Comparative	
bueno/a	*good*	mejor	*better*
malo/a	*bad*	peor	*worse*
grande	*big*	mayor	*bigger*
pequeño/a	*small*	menor	*smaller*
joven	*young*	menor	*younger*
viejo/a	*old*	mayor	*older*

El café es **bueno**. El café es **mejor** que el té.   *Coffee is good.*
Coffee is better than tea.

Adverb		Comparative	
bien	*well*	mejor	*better*
mal	*badly*	peor	*worse*
mucho	*a lot*	más	*more*
poco	*a little*	menos	*less*

Gonzalo toca **bien** el clarinete. Toca el clarinete **mejor** que
Ernesto.   *Gonzalo plays the clarinet well. He plays the
clarinet better than Ernesto does.*

Superlatives

A superlative expresses the highest or lowest degree of a quality.
Use the following constructions to express the superlative in
Spanish. Note that the noun is always preceded by a definite arti-
cle, and that *de* is equivalent to the English *in* or *of*.

▶ definite article + noun + *más* + adjective + *de*

Iris es **la chica más** guapa **de** la clase.   *Iris is the best-looking
girl in the class.*

▶ definite article + noun + *menos* + adjective + *de*

Patricio es **el chico menos** estudioso **de** la clase.   *Patricio is
the least studious boy in the class.*

> **PITFALL!**   *Make sure you use* de *with superlatives and* que *with
> comparatives.*

IRREGULAR SUPERLATIVES

As with comparatives, there are also irregular superlatives. Take a
look at the following chart.

Adjective		Superlative	
bueno/a	*good*	el/la mejor	*the best*
malo/a	*bad*	el/la peor	*the worst*
grande	*big*	el/la mayor	*the biggest*
pequeño/a	*small*	el/la menor	*the smallest*
joven	*young*	el/la menor	*the youngest*
viejo/a	*old*	el/la mayor	*the oldest*

PITFALL! When you use the superlative, make sure your definite article agrees in gender with the noun it accompanies.

Isabel es **la mayor** de su familia. *Isabel is the oldest in her family.*
Yo soy **el mejor** de la clase. *I'm the best in the class.*

ABSOLUTE SUPERLATIVES

If you want to express an even higher degree of quality, you can use the absolute superlative. In Spanish, the absolute superlative is equivalent to "extremely," "exceptionally," or "very" in English.

▶ For adjectives and adverbs that end in a vowel, drop the final vowel and add -*ísimo/a*.

malo ⟶ mal- ⟶ malísimo/a
¡El libro es **malísimo**! *The book is very bad!*

For adjectives and adverbs that end in *c*, *g*, or *z*, make the following spelling changes to the absolute superlative.

c ⟶ *qu* ⟶ -*ísimo/a*
rico ⟶ **riquísimo**

g ⟶ *gu* ⟶ -*ísimo/a*
largo ⟶ **larguísimo**

z ⟶ *c* ⟶ -*ísimo/a*
feliz ⟶ **felicísimo**

▶ For adjectives and adverbs that end in any other consonant, add -ísimo/a.

fácil ⟶ facilísimo/a
¡La lección es **facilísima**!   *The lesson is very easy!*

Prepositions

We learned in Lesson 3 that a preposition expresses the relationship between things in terms of time or place. In other words, prepositions answer questions like "where?" and "when?"

The examples we gave you were:

El lapiz está **en** la mesa.   *The pencil is on the table.*
Te veo **antes de** las 3:00.   *See you before 3:00.*

In the first example, the preposition *en* answers the question "where?" Where is the pencil? It's on the table. In the second example, the preposition *antes de* answers "when?" When will I see you? Before 3:00.

Here are some of the most common prepositions in Spanish.

a	*at, to*	excepto	*except*
ante	*before*	hacia	*toward*
bajo	*under*	hasta	*to, up to, as far as, until*
con	*with*	para	*for*
contra	*against*	por	*for, by*
de	*of, from*	según	*according to*
desde	*from, since*	sin	*without*
durante	*during*	sobre	*on, over, about*
en	*in, into, on, at*	tras	*after*
entre	*between, among*		

LESSON 9

Prepositions cannot stand alone. They must be followed by a noun, pronoun, or a verb in the infinitive. Take a look at these examples.

noun
Salgo **con** Ana.   *I go out with Ana.*

pronoun
Vamos **con** ellos.   *Let's go with them.*

infinitive verb
Hace todo **excepto** cocinar.   *He does everything except cook.*

PRONOUNS AFTER PREPOSITIONS

Here are the pronouns that follow prepositions.

For the singular:

Person		
1st	mí	*me*
2nd	ti	*you*
3rd	él	*him*
	ella	*her*
	usted	*you* (formal)

For the plural:

Person		
1st	nosotros	*us* (masculine)
	nosotras	*us* (feminine)
2nd	vosotros	*you* (plural, masculine)
	vosotras	*you* (plural, feminine)
3rd	ellos	*them* (masculine)
	ellas	*them* (feminine)
	ustedes	*you* (plural, formal)

▶ The preposition *entre* (between) is followed by *tú* and *yo* instead of *ti* and *mí*.

> Hay mucha confianza **entre tú** y **yo**.   *There is a lot of trust between you and me.*

▶ When you combine the preposition *con* with *mí* or *ti*, it becomes *conmigo* or *contigo*.

> ¿Quieres ir **conmigo**?   *Do you want to come with me?*
> Sí, voy **contigo**.   *Yes, I'm going with you.*

Pronouns After Prepositions The pronouns that follow prepositions are exactly the same as the subject pronouns, except for mí and ti.

COMPOUND PREPOSITIONS

Prepositions can be grouped with adverbs or with other prepositions to form a single prepositional expression. Here are some of them.

además de	*in addition to, besides*
antes de	*before*
cerca de	*near, close to*
debajo de	*under, beneath*
delante de	*in front of, before*
dentro de	*inside, within*
después de	*after*
detrás de	*after, behind*
encima de	*on, on top of, over*
enfrente de	*in front of, opposite*
frente a	*in front of, opposite*
fuera de	*outside of, beyond*
lejos de	*far from*
por delante de	*in front of*

Examples:

> Ella está **delante de** mí.   *She is in front of me.*
> Vivo **cerca de** la escuela.   *I live close to school.*
> Las llaves están **encima de** la mesa.   *The keys are on top of the table.*

Prepositions often appear in phrases as well. Take a look at the following prepositional phrases.

a causa de	*because of*
acerca de	*about, concerning*
al lado de	*next to, beside*
en vez de	*instead of*
frente a	*across from, opposite to*

Examples:

> Las tijeras están **al lado del** lápiz.   *The scissors are next to the pencil.*
> Quiero hablar con la profesora **acerca de** mi nota.   *I want to talk to my teacher about my grade.*

INDIVIDUAL PREPOSITIONS

Prepositions are difficult in any language. They must often be memorized. Let's take a look at some of the trickier ones in Spanish.

The Preposition a

We saw the preposition *a* in Lesson 6, when we discussed direct and indirect objects. Use the preposition *a*:

▶ To introduce an indirect object

> Le doy la manzana **a** Josefina.   *I give the apple to Josefina.*

▶ To show movement toward something or some place

> Vamos **a** la cabaña.   *We're going to the cabin.*

▶ To tell the time at which something happens

El concierto es **a** las ocho.   *The concert is at eight o'clock.*

▶ To show distance

La escuela está **a** una cuadra.   *The school is one block away.*

▶ When *alguien, nadie, alguno,* and *ninguno* are direct objects and refer to people (personal *a*)

No veo **a** nadie.   *I don't see anyone.*

▶ To introduce a direct object that refers to a person (personal *a*)

Veo **a** mi hermana.   *I see my sister.*

Certain verbs are often accompanied by the preposition *a*. These are all followed by the verb in the infinitive. Try to learn them.

aprender a + infinitive (to learn to)	**Aprendo a** tocar el piano.
	I learn to play the piano.
ayudar a + infinitive (to help)	Le **ayudo a** mi abuela a preparar la cena.
	I help my grandmother prepare dinner.
comenzar a + infinitive (to begin to)	**Comienza a** llover.
	It starts to rain.
enseñar a + infinitive (to teach)	Te **enseño a** cantar.
	I teach you to sing.
invitar a + infinitive (to invite to)	Le **invito a** ir al cine.
	I invite him/her to go to the movies.

The Preposition de

Use the preposition *de*:

▶ To show possession

La camisa es **de** Marta.   *The shirt is Marta's.*

▶ To show origin

Soy **de** los Estados Unidos.   *I'm from the United States.*

LESSON 9

▶ To show the material that something is made of

El plato es **de** plástico.   *The plate is made of plastic.*

▶ To describe someone by a physical trait

La señora **de** los ojos azules es mi madre.   *The woman with blue eyes is my mother.*

Here are some verbs with *de.*

acabar de + infinitive (to have just [done something])	**Acabo de** comer. *I just ate.*
dejar de + infinitive (to stop)	Quiero **dejar de** mentir. *I want to stop lying.*
pensar de (to think of or about)	¿Qué **piensas del** libro? *What do you think about the book?*
terminar de + infinitive (to finish)	**Termino de** lavar los platos. *I finish washing the dishes.*
tratar de + infinitive (to try to)	**Trata de** ayudarme. *He/She tries to help me.*

THE PREPOSITIONS PARA AND POR

The prepositions *para* and *por* can both be translated as "for." However, they have different uses in Spanish.

The Preposition para

Use the preposition *para:*

▶ To indicate a particular use for which something is intended

Las piernas son **para** caminar.   *Legs are for walking.*

▶ To show the destination for which something is intended

El regalo es **para** mi padre. *The gift is for my father.*

▶ With an infinitive that expresses the purpose of something

Para comer, necesito un tenedor.   *To eat, I need a fork.*

▸ To indicate a deadline or a time at which something will be fulfilled

> La entrada es **para** el concierto del domingo.   *The ticket is for the concert on Sunday.*

▸ To indicate a comparison of inequality with something that is different from what is expected

> **Para** extranjero, habla bien el español.   *For a foreigner, he speaks Spanish well*

The Preposition *por*

Use the preposition *por*:

▸ To indicate a length of time during which an action takes place

> ¿Me prestas el carro **por** dos días?   *Will you lend me the car for two days?*

▸ To indicate movement through or along something

> El gato pasa **por** la ventana.   *The cat goes through the window.*

▸ To indicate the means by which something is communicated

> Te llamo **por** teléfono.   *I call you on the phone.*

▸ After the verbs *ir* (to go), *mandar* (to send), *enviar* (to mail), *volver* (to return), *regresar* (to come back), *preguntar* (to ask for) when there is an object of an errand

> Te mando el paquete **por** avión.   *I send you the package airmail.*

▸ To indicate the reason for an action

> Estoy en la universidad **por** mis padres.   *I'm at the university for the sake of my parents.*

▶ To indicate a substitution (*instead of*)

    Yo corro **por** Manuel.   *I'm running in Manuel's place.*

▶ To indicate an exchange of one thing for another

    Te doy diez dólares **por** la chaqueta.   *I'll give you ten dollars for the jacket.*

▶ To indicate a rate

    El carro va ochenta a kilómetros **por** hora.   *The car goes eighty kilometers per hour.*

VERBS WITHOUT PREPOSITIONS

The following verbs have prepositions in English but not in Spanish.

agradecer (to be grateful for)	Te agradezco la ayuda.
	*I'm grateful to you **for** your help.*
buscar (to look for)	Busco mis llaves.
	*I'm looking **for** my keys.*
esperar (to wait for)	Los niños esperan el bus.
	*The kids are waiting **for** the bus.*
pedir + thing (to ask for something)	Pido un refresco.
	*I ask **for** a drink.*
pensar + infinitive (to plan on doing something)	Pienso ir a la playa.
	*I'm planning **on** going to the beach.*

Functional Language: Using ¿qué? and ¿cuál?

In Lesson 3, we learned how to form a question. We also learned how to use question words, such as *¿qué?* and *¿cuál?* Let's learn a little bit more about how to ask "what?" or "which?" in Spanish.

Both *¿qué?* and *¿cuál(-es)?* can be used with the verb *ser* and mean *what?* or *which?* However, they are used in different situations.

¿QUÉ?

▶ *¿Qué?* is used with the verb *ser* when asking for a definition or an identification.

> **¿Qué** es esto?   *What is this?*
> Es una torta.   *It's a cake.*

> **¿Qué** es una torta?   *What's a cake?*
> Es un postre.   *It's a dessert.*

▶ When *¿qué?* is followed by a noun, it means "which."

> **¿Qué** cuadro te gustó más?   *Which painting did you like the most?*

¿CUÁL?

▶ *¿Cuál?* and *¿cuáles?* are used with the verb *ser* when there is a choice among several possibilities.

> **¿Cuál** es tu película favorita?   *What is your favorite movie?*
> **¿Cuáles** son tus mejores juegos?   *What are your best games?*

▶ *¿Cuál?* and *¿cuáles?* can also be used with verbs other than *ser.*

> **¿Cuáles** libros has leído?   *Which books have you read?*

Sample Test Questions

PART 1, Exercise A

Fill in the blanks with the correct comparative word. Use the cues in parentheses.

1. Emilia mira _____ televisión que Cristina. (more)

2. Tú eres _____ simpática que Catalina. (less)

3. No estudio _____ tú. (as much as)

4. Conocen _____ canciones que yo. (more)

5. Mi escuela es _____ que su escuela. (better)

6. Tu comes _____ comida como Ricardo. (as much)

7. La manzana es _____ rica que la banana. (less)

8. El hermano de Daniel es _____ que él. (younger)

9. La música clásica es _____ que el rock. (worse)

10. Mis padres tienen _____ dinero que mis tíos. (more)

Exercise B

Turn the following adjectives into superlatives. Use the cues: for +, use *most*, and for –, use *least*.

1. niño paciente _____ (+)

2. señora diplomática _____ (–)

3. chica inteligente _____ (–)

4. libro bueno _____ (+)

5. abuela vieja _____ (–)

6. *hombre malo* _____ (+)

7. *ejercicio fácil* _____ (+)

8. *carro rápido* _____ (–)

9. *casa pequeña* _____ (+)

10. *camisa cara* _____ (–)

Exercise C

Turn the adjectives into absolute superlatives. Rewrite the sentences.

1. *El pan es rico.*

_____

2. *La niña es traviesa.*

_____

3. *El profesor es malo.*

_____

4. *La calle (road) es larga.*

_____

5. *Estoy feliz.*

_____

PART 2, Exercise A

Use the following compound prepositions to express where the cat is: *delante de, debajo de, encima de, dentro de, lejos de.* Write in complete sentences.

1. _____

2. _____
   _____
   _____
   _____

3. _____

4. _____

_____

_____

_____

5. _____

Exercise B

Choose the correct preposition. Circle the letter.

1. *La mesa es _____ madera* (wood).

    A. a
    B. de
    C. no preposition

2. *Mando un mensaje a Arturo _____ correo electrónico.* (email)

    A. para
    B. por
    C. en

3. *La mantequilla* (butter) *es _____ el pan.*

    A. para
    B. por
    C. en

4. ¿Buscas _____ la clase de español?

    A. a
    B. para
    C. no preposition

5. La película (movie) es _____ las tres de la tarde.

    A. de
    B. por
    C. a

6. Ignacio corre _____ la esquina (corner).

    A. por
    B. hasta
    C. no preposition

7. Espero _____ mi amiga Carla.

    A. a
    B. de
    C. no preposition

8. La caja (box) es _____ los lápices.

    A. por
    B. con
    C. para

PART 3, Exercise A

Fill in the blank with ¿qué? or ¿cuál(-es)?

1. ¿_____ es tu clase favorita?

2. ¿_____ es un "disco compacto"?

3. ¿_____ son los platos más ricos?

4. ¿_____ es eso?

5. ¿_____ de las dos es menos cara?

Exercise B

Translate the following questions into Spanish.

1. *What is your favorite song?*

   _____

2. *Which joke (broma) is funnier?*

   _____

3. *Which shirt do you like?*

   _____

4. *Which one do you want?*

   _____

5. *What is that?*

   _____

LESSON 9

Lesson 10

Imperfect Tense of Verbs
- Regular Verbs
- Irregular Verbs

Preterite Tense vs. Imperfect Tense
- Use the Preterite Tense
- Use the Imperfect Tense
- Use Both the Preterite and the Imperfect
- Special Verbs in the Preterite vs. Imperfect Tenses

Functional Language:
  Talking About Continuous Actions in the Past (Past Progressive)

Sample Test Questions

10

Imperfect Tense of Verbs

You have already learned how to use the preterite tense to express actions and events in the past. The preterite, as you know, is used to express actions that are finished or complete.

The imperfect is the second kind of simple past tense. In contrast to the preterite, the imperfect expresses actions or events that are continuous or habitual in the past. The imperfect is also used for describing the past. We'll go into more detail at the end of the lesson.

The imperfect has several equivalents in English. For example, *corría* (the first-person singular imperfect form of *correr*) can mean "I ran," "I was running," "I would run," or "I used to run."

REGULAR VERBS

Luckily, all but three verbs are regular in the imperfect. Here are the conjugations.

-ar Verbs

For singular *-ar* verbs, add *-aba*, *-abas*, and *-aba*.

Person	Singular	
1st	yo cantaba	*I sang*
2nd	tú cantabas	*you sang*
3rd	él cantaba	*he sang*
	ella cantaba	*she sang*
	usted cantaba	*you sang* (formal)

Conjugating the Imperfect Note that the first-person singular and the third-person singular are the same.

For plural -*ar* verbs, add -*ábamos*, -*abais*, and -*aban*.

Person	Plural	
1st	nosotros cantábamos	*we were singing* (masculine)
	nosotras cantábamos	*we were singing* (feminine)
2nd	vosotros cantabais	*you were singing* (plural, masculine)
	vosotras cantabais	*you were singing* (plural, feminine)
3rd	ellos cantaban	*they sang* (masculine)
	ellas cantaban	*they sang* (feminine)
	ustedes cantaban	*you sang* (plural, formal)

-er and -ir Verbs

For singular -*er* and -*ir* verbs, add -*ía*, -*ías*, and -*ía*.

Person	Singular	
1st	yo comía	*I was eating*
2nd	tú comías	*you were eating*
3rd	él comía	*he ate*
	ella comía	*she ate*
	usted comía	*you ate* (formal)

Person	Singular	
1st	yo escribía	*I was writing*
2nd	tú escribías	*you were writing*
3rd	él escribía	*he wrote*
	ella escribía	*she wrote*
	usted escribía	*you wrote* (formal)

For plural -*er* and -*ir* verbs, add -*íamos*, -*íais*, and -*ían*.

Person	Plural	
1st	nosotros comíamos	*we were eating* (masculine)
	nosotras comíamos	*we were eating* (feminine)
2nd	vosotros comíais	*you were eating* (plural, masculine)
	vosotras comíais	*you were eating* (plural, feminine)
3rd	ellos comían	*they ate* (masculine)
	ellas comían	*they ate* (feminine)
	ustedes comían	*you ate* (plural, formal)

LESSON 10

Person	Plural	
1st	nosotros escribíamos	*we were writing* (masculine)
	nosotras escribíamos	*we were writing* (feminine)
2nd	vosotros escribíais	*you were writing* (plural, masculine)
	vosotras escribíais	*you were writing* (plural, feminine)
3rd	ellos escribían	*they wrote* (masculine)
	ellas escribían	*they wrote* (feminine)
	ustedes escribían	*you wrote* (plural, formal)

IRREGULAR VERBS

As mentioned earlier, there are only three verbs that have irregular forms in the imperfect tense: *ir*, *ser*, and *ver*. You've seen these verbs before, and they've always been irregular, so this shouldn't come as too big of a surprise.

ir (to go)		
Person	**Singular**	
1st	yo iba	*I was going*
2nd	tú ibas	*you were going*
3rd	él iba	*he went*
	ella iba	*she went*
	usted iba	*you went* (formal)
Person	**Plural**	
1st	nosotros íbamos	*we were going* (masculine)
	nosotras íbamos	*we were going* (feminine)
2nd	vosotros ibais	*you were going* (plural, masculine)
	vosotras ibais	*you were going* (plural, feminine)
3rd	ellos iban	*they went* (masculine)
	ellas iban	*they went* (feminine)
	ustedes iban	*you went* (plural, formal)

ser (to be)		
Person	**Singular**	
1st	yo era	*I was*
2nd	tú eras	*you were*
3rd	él era	*he was*
	ella era	*she was*
	usted era	*you were* (formal)
Person	**Plural**	
1st	nosotros éramos	*we were* (masculine)
	nosotras éramos	*we were* (feminine)
2nd	vosotros erais	*you were* (plural, masculine)
	vosotras erais	*you were* (plural, feminine)
3rd	ellos eran	*they were* (masculine)
	ellas eran	*they were* (feminine)
	ustedes eran	*you were* (plural, formal)

ver (to see)		
Person	**Singular**	
1st	yo veía	*I was seeing*
2nd	tú veías	*you were seeing*
3rd	él veía	*he saw*
	ella veía	*she saw*
	usted veía	*you saw* (formal)
Person	**Plural**	
1st	nosotros veíamos	*we were seeing* (masculine)
	nosotras veíamos	*we were seeing* (feminine)
2nd	vosotros veíais	*you were seeing* (plural, masculine)
	vosotras veíais	*you were seeing* (plural, feminine)
3rd	ellos veían	*they saw* (masculine)
	ellas veían	*they saw* (feminine)
	ustedes veían	*you saw* (plural, formal)

Preterite Tense vs. Imperfect Tense

Once you have determined that you need to use a past tense, you have to decide whether to use the preterite or the imperfect. To do this, try to visualize the perspective given to the verb in its specific context. In other words, think about the action of the verb.

USE THE PRETERITE TENSE

▶ Does the verb express an action that has a specific ending? Did the action happen? In this case, use the preterite tense.

> La hermana de Paul **se casó** el año pasado.   *Paul's sister got married last year.*

In the sentence above, the verb is in the preterite tense. The action of Paul's sister getting married happened at that moment, and was then over.

▶ Does the verb express the specific beginning or end of a past action? Then use the preterite tense.

> La clase **empezó** a las diez.   *The class started at 10.*
> Ayer **terminé** mi tarea de física.   *Yesterday I finished my physics homework.*

In the first sentence, the class had a specific start time: 10:00. In the second sentence, the homework was finished at a specific time: yesterday.

▶ Does the verb narrate a series of past actions or events? Then use the preterite tense. Take a look at the following sentence.

> La profesora **entró** a la clase, **abrió** su libro, y **escribió** en la pizarra.   *The professor entered the room, opened her book, and wrote on the chalkboard.*

In the sentence above, the verbs are in the preterite tense. *Entró*, *abrió*, and *escribió* all belong to a series of events initiated by *la profesora*.

Preterite Cues

Certain words and expressions are often associated with the preterite tense. These are:

ayer	*yesterday*
anteayer	*the day before yesterday*
una vez	*once*
dos veces	*twice*
el año pasado	*last year*
el martes pasado	*last Tuesday (etc.)*
de repente	*suddenly*

PITFALL! *These words do not automatically indicate the preterite tense. Be sure to consider the context of the verb before conjugating it.*

Verbs That Use the Preterite Tense Punctual verbs like salir, entrar, recordar, empezar, terminar, llegar, and caerse are almost always in the preterite because they represent actions that don't take any time.

USE THE IMPERFECT TENSE

▶ Does the verb express an action that was habitual? Was the action ongoing? Then use the imperfect tense.

Carla **caminaba** todas las tardes por una hora.   *Carla walked/used to walk for an hour every afternoon.*

In the sentence above, the verb is in the imperfect tense. The action was habitual: Carla walked every afternoon for an hour.

▶ Does the verb describe an ongoing past event with no definite beginning or end? Then use the imperfect tense.

María Clara **corría** en la pista.   *María Clara ran/was running/used to run on the track.*

In the sentence above, the verb is in the imperfect tense. The action (running) continued over a span of time in the past, but had no definite start or end.

> **PITFALL!** Corría *could mean three things: "ran," "was running," or "used to run." In such a case, context would clarify the verb's meaning.*

▶ Does the verb describe a mental, physical, or emotional state or condition? Then use the imperfect tense.

La mujer se **sentía** enferma.   *The woman felt / was feeling ill.*
La casa **tenía** tres pisos.   *The house had three floors.*

In both sentences, the verb is in the imperfect because it expresses a physical condition. The first sentence expresses how the woman was feeling; the second expresses how many floors the house had.

▶ Does the verb express someone's age in the past? Then use the imperfect tense.

En 1996, mi hermana **tenía** 15 años.   *In 1996, my sister was 15.*

> **Verbs That Use the Imperfect Tense** *Non-action verbs like* amar, ser, estar, desear, parecer, tener, *and* hacer, *in weather expressions, are generally used to give background information and almost always take the imperfect.*

Imperfect Cues

As with the preterite tense, certain words and expressions are often associated with the imperfect tense. These are:

todas las tardes	*every afternoon*
todos los martes	*every Tuesday (etc.)*
siempre	*always*
mientras	*while*
frecuentemente	*often*
de niño	*as a child*

> **PITFALL!** *These words do not automatically indicate the imperfect tense. Be sure you think about the context of the verb before conjugating it.*

USE BOTH THE PRETERITE AND THE IMPERFECT

In some cases, you can use both the preterite and the imperfect tenses in the same sentence. In this case, the imperfect tense describes what was happening, while the preterite tense describes the interruption.

what was happening   interrupting action

Catalina **hablaba** por teléfono cuando **sonó** el timbre.
Catalina was speaking on the phone when the doorbell rang.

In the sentence above, the action of the doorbell ringing interrupted Catalina's talking.

> **General vs. Specific** *Here's another way to think about the decision to use imperfect or preterite: general actions correspond to the imperfect tense, for example, daily walking (no particular day or walk being referred to). Specific actions correspond to the preterite tense: a particular walk on a particular day.*

Preterite and Imperfect in the Presentation of an Event

Sometimes you will see the preterite and the imperfect tenses together in the presentation of an event: for example in a news or fictional story. In these cases, the imperfect tense gives us all the background information (such as the time, mood, location, and weather), while the preterite tense tells us what happened. Take a look at the following narrative.

> **Era** medianoche, y **caía** la lluvia. **Hacía** mucho frío, pero **salí** de todas maneras. De repente, **me resbalé** en un charco de agua y **caí** en la vereda. ¡Ay!
>
> *It was midnight, and it was raining. It was very cold, but I went out anyway. Suddenly, I slipped on a puddle of water and fell on the sidewalk. Ouch!*

SPECIAL VERBS IN THE PRETERITE VS. IMPERFECT TENSES

In Lesson 8, we discussed verbs that change meaning when used in the preterite tense. When used in the imperfect tense, the verbs maintain their original, present-tense meanings.

▶ As we learned, when *saber* is in the preterite tense, it means "found out."

> **Supo** que su primo murió.   *He found out that his cousin died.*

When *saber* is in the imperfect tense, it means "knew."

> **Sabía** francés cuando era niño.   *He knew French when he was a child.*

▶ When *conocer* is in the preterite tense, it means "met for the first time."

> **Conocí** a Magdalena en la fiesta.   *I met Magdalena at the party.*

When *conocer* is in the imperfect tense, it means "knew."

> **Conocíamos** a la familia García.   *We knew the García family.*

▶ When *querer* is in the preterite tense, it can either mean "attempted" or "refused to."

> **Quiso** escapar, pero no pudo.   *He attempted to escape, but he couldn't.*

When *querer* is in the imperfect tense, it means "wanted."

Queríamos viajar. *We wanted to travel.*
No **quiso** ayudarme. *He refused to help me.*

Functional Language: Talking About Continuous Actions in the Past (Past Progressive)

In Lesson 6, we learned about the present progressive. The present progressive is formed with the present tense of *estar*, plus the present participle (*estamos comiendo, estás llorando*, etc.).

Another way to talk about ongoing actions in the past is to use the **past progressive**.

The past progressive is formed with the imperfect tense of *estar* plus the present participle.

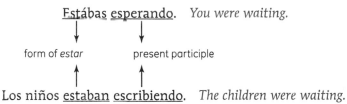

Estábas esperando. *You were waiting.*

form of *estar*   present participle

Los niños estaban escribiendo. *The children were waiting.*

Note that a simple imperfect can also be used to express ongoing actions.

Esperabas. *You were waiting.*
Los niños **escribían**. *The children were writing.*

However, the use of the progressive emphasizes that the action was actually in progress at the time.

Sample Test Questions

PART 1, Exercise A

Conjugate the following verbs in the imperfect tense.

1. Vosotros _____ (ir).

2. Tú _____(recibir).

3. Lo _____ (ser).

4. Los estudiantes _____ (leer).

5. Vosotros _____ (ver).

6. Ellas _____ (correr).

7. Mis padres _____ (ir).

8. Vosotras _____ (ser).

9. Tú _____ (tener).

10. Nosotros _____ (llegar).

Exercise B

Fill in the blanks with the imperfect form of the verb in parentheses.

1. Magdalena _____ (ver) la televisión todos los días.

2. El año pasado (las year), mis tareas _____ (ser) muy difíciles.

3. José se _____ (aburrir) en la clase de español.

4. Francisco me _____ (esperar) en el gimnasio.

5. En 1997, nosotros _____ (ser) muy pequeños.

6. *Hace veinte años* (twenty years ago), *mi ciudad* _____
   (ser) más limpia (clean).

7. *El verano pasado* (last summer) *vosotros* _____ *(leer)*
   todos los días.

8. *Tú siempre* _____ *(mandar) cartas a tus abuelos.*

9. *Los niños se* _____ *(bañar) en la piscina* (swimming pool).

10. *Cuando yo* _____ *(vivir) en Quito, yo* _____ *(ir)*
    siempre a la Mitad del Mundo.

PART 2, Exercise A

Choose the verb tense based on the context of the sentence.
Write the answer in the space provided.

1. *Todos los días, los novios* _____ *juntos.*

   A. almorzaron
   B. almorzaban

2. *Francisco y yo* _____ *al parque ayer.*

   A. íbamos
   B. fuimos

3. *Hoy* _____ *a casa a las dos de la tarde.*

   A. regresamos
   B. regresábamos

4. *Cristina tocaba la guitarra cuando* _____ *el teléfono.*

   A. sonaba
   B. sonó

5. *La profesora* _____ *la lección.*

   A. comenzó
   B. comenzaba

LESSON 10

6. Llegué a casa, comí, y _____ mi libro.

    A. leía
    B. leí

Exercise B

Fill in the blank with the preterite or imperfect tense of the verb in parentheses.

1. Esta mañana Paco _____ (levantarse) temprano.

2. Cuando yo _____ (ser) niña, _____ (creer) en Papá Noél (Santa Claus).

3. Para mi cumpleaños María me _____ (dar) una blusa azul.

4. De repente _____ (empezar) a llover.

5. El niño _____ (llorar) todas las noches.

6. Cuando yo _____ (entrar) al cuarto, _____ (ver) a mi hermano.

7. En los años sesenta ese hombre _____ (ser) un cantante famoso.

8. Ayer Nancy _____ (comer) una ensalada.

9. El profesor _____ (olvidar) su pluma en la clase.

10. _____ (hacer) mucho frío cuando fuimos al parque.

Exercise C

Translate the following sentences into Spanish. On the first line, use the past progressive. On the second line, use the simple imperfect.

1. *We were eating in the kitchen.*

   a. _____

   b. _____

2. *The students were studying Spanish.*

   a. _____

   b. _____

3. *My mother was cooking.*

   a. _____

   b. _____

4. *You were traveling in South America.*

   a. _____

   b. _____

5. *You (plural) were listening to the radio.*

   a. _____

   b. _____

LESSON 10

Lesson 11

Adverbs
- *-mente* Adverbs
- Adverbs That Answer Questions
- Multiple-Function Words

Constructions with *Se*
- Impersonal *Se*
- *Se* for Unintentional Actions

Introduction to the Subjunctive
- The Subjunctive in English
- Present Subjunctive of Regular Verbs
- Present Subjunctive of Irregular Verbs
- Uses of the Subjunctive

Functional Language: Constructions with *Hace*

Sample Test Questions

Adverbs

In Lesson 3, we briefly explained the function of adverbs: to modify verbs, adjectives, or other adverbs. Here are some examples of adverbs.

Antonieta habla **bien**.   *Antonieta speaks well.*
(verb)

Eres **muy** bonita.   *You are very pretty.*
(adjective)

> **Adverb Placement** *An adverb precedes the adjective it modifies but normally follows the verb it modifies.*

adverb   adjective
El profesor us **muy** inteligente.   *The teacher is very intelligent.*

verb   adverb
Ellos juegan **bien**.   *They play well.*

-MENTE ADVERBS

There are several kinds of adverbs in Spanish. The easiest adverbs are those that end in *-mente*. Think of *-mente* as the English suffix *-ly*.

To form a *-mente* adverb, simply add *-mente* to the feminine form of the adjective.

Adjective ⟶ Feminine + *-mente*
lento ⟶ lenta ⟶ lentamente   *slowly*

Remember that the masculine and feminine forms of some adjectives are the same. In this case add *-mente* to the base form of the adjective.

Adjective + *-mente*
alegre ⟶ alegremente   *happily*

▶ When you put together a string of *-mente* adverbs, drop the ending for all but the last one. Take a look at this example.

La profesora habla **clara** y **lentamente**.   *The teacher speaks clarly and slowly.*

ADVERBS THAT ANSWER QUESTIONS

Other adverbs are not as easy to remember, because they don't follow the *-mente* pattern. These require memorization. However, it will be easier if you think of them as answering the questions *¿cómo?*, *¿dónde?*, *¿cuándo?*, and *¿cuánto?*

Adverbs of Manner

¿Cómo? adverbs answer the question "how?" These adverbs are also called "adverbs of manner."

Question:
¿<u>Cómo</u> cocinas?   *How do you cook?*

Answer:
Cocino **bien**.   *I cook well.*

> **PITFALL!**   Be careful with bien and bueno. Bien is an adjective, but bueno is an adverb.

Other adverbs like *bien*:

Adverbs of Manner	
así	*like that, thus*
de pronto	*suddenly*
mal	*badly*
menos	*less*
más	*more*

Adverbs of Place

¿Dónde? adverbs answer the question "where?" These adverbs are also called "adverbs of place."

Question:
¿<u>Dónde</u> está la escuela?   *Where is the school?*

Answer:
La escuela está cerca.   *The school is close.*

Other adverbs like *cerca*:

Adverbs of Place	
abajo	*below*
acá	*over here*
adelante	*in front*
adentro	*inside*
aquí	*here*
allá	*over there*
arriba	*above*
debajo	*underneath*
delante	*in front*
detrás	*behind*
encima	*on top*
lejos	*far*

You have seen many of these words before. These phrasal prepositions also function as adverbs because they modify verbs of location (usually *estar*).

Adverbs of Time

¿Cuándo? adverbs answer the question "when?" These adverbs are also called "adverbs of time."

Question:
¿<u>Cuándo</u> vas al aeropuerto? *When are you going to the airport?*

Answer:
Voy **pronto** al aeropuerto. *I'm going to the airport soon.*

Other adverbs like *pronto*:

Adverbs of Time	
Times of day	
ahora	*now*
hoy	*today*
anoche	*last night*
ayer	*yesterday*
mañana	*tomorrow*
de día	*during the day*
de noche	*at night*
a la una (a las dos, etc.)	*at one o'clock (at two, etc.)*
Others	
a veces	*sometimes*
antes	*before*
después	*after*
entonces	*then*
luego	*later*
mientras	*while*
nunca	*never*
siempre	*always*
tarde	*late*
temprano	*early*
todavía	*still*
ya	*already*

Adverbs of Quantity

¿Cuánto? adverbs answer the question "how much?" These adverbs are also called "adverbs of quantity."

Question:
¿Cuánto habla Patricia? *How much does Patricia talk?*

Answer:
¡Patricia habla **demasiado**! *Patricia talks too much!*

Other adverbs like *demasiado*:

Adverbs of Quantity	
algo	*a bit, rather*
apenas	*barely*
bastante	*a lot*
casi	*almost*
cuanto	*as much*
más	*more*
medio	*half, somewhat*
menos	*less*
mucho	*a lot*
muy	*very*
nada	*not at all*
poco	*a little*
sólo	*only*
tanto	*so much*

Adverbs of Confirmation, Negation, and Doubt

Adverbs can also be used to confirm, negate, and express doubt. These are called "adverbs of confirmation," "adverbs of negation," and "adverbs of doubt." Take a look at the following chart.

Adverbs of Confirmation	
claro	*of course*
sí	*yes*
sin duda	*without a doubt*
por supuesto	*of course*
ya	*already*
Adverbs of Negation	
no	*no*
tampoco	*neither*
claro que no	*of course not*
Adverbs of Doubt	
acaso	*perhaps, maybe*
tal vez	*maybe*
quizás	*maybe*

MULTIPLE-FUNCTION WORDS

Some words can be adverbs or adjectives, depending on their function in the sentence.

Comen **mucho** queso.   *They eat a lot of cheese.*

Corren **mucho**.   *They run a lot.*

In the first sentence, *mucho* modifies *queso* and is an adjective. In the second sentence, *mucho* modifies *corren* and is an adverb.

There is one important difference between adjectives and adverbs: adjectives change in gender and number along with the nouns they modify, but adverbs do not. If you were to make the noun plural in the first sentence, *mucho* would have to change too.

Comen **muchos** quesos.   *They eat a lot of cheeses.*

In addition, if *mucho/s* were to modify a feminine noun, it would have to change to *mucha/s*.

Julieta tiene **mucha** ropa.   *Julieta has a lot of clothes.*

> **PITFALL!**   *Be careful with* mucho *and* muy. Mucho *is an adjective, but* muy *is an adverb.*

Other words like *mucho*:

poco   *a little*
bastante   *a lot*
mal   *bad*

Constructions with Se

We learned a little about the word *se* in Lesson 8, when we covered reflexive verbs. *Se*, as we now know, is the third-person reflexive pronoun.

Se has other important uses.

IMPERSONAL SE

Se can be used to make impersonal statements. Such statements do not specify who is doing the action.

▶ In impersonal statements, *se* is used with the third-person singular form of the verb and can be translated as "one," "they," "people," or "you."

> **Se** come bien en este restaurante.   *One eats well at this restaurant.*

▶ The third-person plural of the verb may also be used to make an impersonal statement.

> **Dicen** que el restaurante es bueno.   *They say that the restaurant is good.*

or

> **Se** dice que el restaurante es bueno.   *They say that the restaurant is good.*

SE FOR UNINTENTIONAL ACTIONS

Se can also be used to express an action that occurred unintentionally. It is especially useful when the doer doesn't want to take responsibility for what happened. In these cases, the construction stresses that the action was accidental.

▶ To form this kind of statement, use the following pattern: *se* + indirect object pronoun + verb + subject.

> Se le **rompieron** las **gafas**.   *His/her sunglasses got broken.*
> ¿Se te **dañaron** los **pantalones**?   *Were your pants ruined?*

indirect object
pronoun
       subject
    | |
  verb

Se me perdió el libro.   *My book got lost.*

> **PITFALL!**   *Be sure that the verb agrees in number with the subject.*

Se nos **olvidó** ir a la **fiesta**.   *We forgot to go to the party.*

▶ If you want to state who is performing the action, use the construction: *a* + noun or *a* + prepositional pronoun.

A <u>Teodoro</u> se le cayó el libro.   *Teodoro dropped his book.*
A <u>mí</u> se me perdió el lápiz.   *I lost the pencil.*

Introduction to the Subjunctive

Verbs can be in three moods: indicative, subjunctive, and imperative. So far, all the verbs you have learned have been in the indicative mood. The indicative mood is used to state facts and to talk about actions that are real and definite. Now we will introduce another mood, the subjunctive.

The subjunctive, as opposed to the indicative, doesn't deal with factual reality but rather with feelings, opinions, suppositions, dreams, and speculations. That sounds pretty vague. The truth is, the subjunctive is challenging for anyone. You'll learn more about it and the imperative mood (commands) in your next Spanish course. For this reason, we'll only introduce the subjunctive in this book.

THE SUBJUNCTIVE IN ENGLISH

Many people say that there isn't really a subjunctive in English. This isn't true. Look at the following sentences:

▸ My grandmother's doctor recommended that she **drink** six glasses of water a day.

▸ If I **were** the class president, I'd let students out an hour early.

▸ The law requires that you **be** 18 years old to vote.

In the three sentences above, you'll see that the verbs *drink*, *were*, and *be* are conjugated differently than expected (she drink vs. she drinks, I were vs. I am, and you be vs. you are). These are three examples of the subjunctive in English. It's true, however, that the subjunctive mood is used only rarely in English. In Spanish, it is used very frequently, and it is necessary for you to learn it.

PRESENT SUBJUNCTIVE OF REGULAR VERBS

This is how to conjugate the present subjunctive of regular *-ar,-er*, and *-ir* verbs.

For singular *-ar* verbs, add *-e*, *-es*, and *-e* to the stem.

Person	Singular	
1st	yo cante	*I sing*
2nd	tú cantes	*you sing*
3rd	él cante	*he sings*
	ella cante	*she sings*
	usted cante	*you sing* (formal)

For plural *-ar* verbs, add *-emos*, *-éis*, and *-en* to the stem.

Person	Plural	
1st	nosotros cantemos	*we sing* (masculine)
	nosotras cantemos	*we sing* (feminine)
2nd	vosotros cantéis	*you sing* (plural, masculine)
	vosotras cantéis	*you sing* (plural, feminine)
3rd	ellos canten	*they sing* (masculine)
	ellas canten	*they sing* (feminine)
	ustedes canten	*you sing* (plural, formal)

For singular -er and -ir verbs, add -a, -as, and -a to the verb stem.

Person	Singular	
1st	yo coma	*I eat*
2nd	tú comas	*you eat*
3rd	él coma	*he eats*
	ella coma	*she eats*
	usted coma	*you eat* (formal)

Person	Singular	
1st	yo escriba	*I write*
2nd	tú escribas	*you write*
3rd	él escriba	*he writes*
	ella escriba	*she writes*
	usted escriba	*you write* (formal)

For plural -er and -ir verbs, add -amos, -áis, and -an to the stem.

Person	Plural	
1st	nosotros comemas	*we eat* (masculine)
	nosotras comemas	*we eat* (feminine)
2nd	vosotros comáis	*you eat* (plural, masculine)
	vosotras comáis	*you eat* (plural, feminine)
3rd	ellos coman	*they eat* (masculine)
	ellas coman	*they eat* (feminine)
	ustedes coman	*you eat* (plural, formal)

Person	Plural	
1st	nosotros escribamos	*we write* (masculine)
	nosotras escribamos	*we write* (feminine)
2nd	vosotros escribáis	*you write* (plural, masculine)
	vosotras escribáis	*you write* (plural, feminine)
3rd	ellos escriban	*they write* (masculine)
	ellas escriban	*they write* (feminine)
	ustedes escriban	*you write* (plural, formal)

Present Subjunctive of Stem-Changing Verbs

▶ Verbs with irregular *yo* forms show the same irregularities in the present subjunctive.

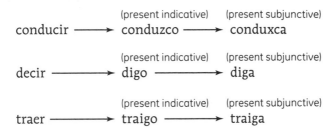

conducir ——→ conduzco ——→ conduxca
(present indicative) (present subjunctive)

decir ——→ digo ——————→ diga
(present indicative) (present subjunctive)

traer ——————→ traigo ——→ traiga
(present indicative) (present subjunctive)

▶ Stem-changing *-ar* and *-er* verbs have the same stem changes in the subjunctive as in the present indicative.

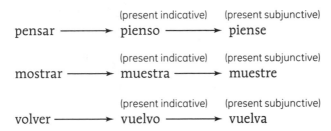

pensar ——————→ pienso ——→ piense
(present indicative) (present subjunctive)

mostrar ——→ muestra ——→ muestre
(present indicative) (present subjunctive)

volver ——————→ vuelvo ——→ vuelva
(present indicative) (present subjunctive)

▶ Stem-changing *-ir* have the same stem changes in the subjunctive, except that the nosotros/nosotras and vosotros/vosotras forms have a change as well: from *e* to *i*, and from *o* to *u*.

pedir ——→ pido ——→ pida ——→ pidamos ——→ pidaís
(nosotros, subjunctive) (vosotros, subjunctive)

dormir ——→ duermo ——→ duerma ——→ durmamos ——→ durmaís
(nosotros, subjunctive) (vosotros, subjunctive)

PRESENT SUBJUNCTIVE OF IRREGULAR VERBS

These six verbs are irregular in the present subjunctive.

dar (to give)

Person	Singular	Plural
1st	yo dé	nosotros demos
		nosotras demos
2nd	tu des	vosotros deis
		vosotras deis
3rd	él dé	ellos den
	ella dé	ellas den
	usted dé	ustedes den

estar (to be)

Person	Singular	Plural
1st	yo esté	nosotros estemos
		nosotras estemos
2nd	tu estés	vosotros estéis
		vosotras estéis
3rd	él esté	ellos estén
	ella esté	ellas estén
	usted esté	ustedes estén

haber (to have)

Person	Singular	Plural
1st	yo haya	nosotros hayamos
		nosotras hayamos
2nd	tu haya	vosotros hayáis
		vosotras hayáis
3rd	él haya	ellos hayan
	ella haya	ellas hayan
	usted haya	ustedes hayan

ir (to go)

Person	Singular	Plural
1st	yo vaya	nosotros vayamos
		nosotras vayamos
2nd	tu vayas	vosotros vayáis
		vosotras vayáis
3rd	él vaya	ellos vayan
	ella vaya	ellas vayan
	usted vaya	ustedes vaya

saber (to know)

Person	Singular	Plural
1st	yo sepa	nosotros sepamos
		nosotras sepamos
2nd	tu sepas	vosotros sepáis
		vosotras sepáis
3rd	él sepa	ellos sepan
	ella sepa	ellas sepan
	usted sepa	ustedes sepan

ser (to be)

Person	Singular	Plural
1st	yo sea	nosotros seamos
		nosotras seamos
2nd	tu seas	vosotros seáis
		vosotras seáis
3rd	él sea	ellos sean
	ella sea	ellas sean
	usted sea	ustedes sean

USES OF THE SUBJUNCTIVE

The subjunctive is often used in complex sentences that contain a main clause and a subordinate clause, separated by the word *que*.

Use the subjunctive in the following situations. Note the connector, *que*.

▶ With a verb that gives advice or indicates a desire or wish

(gives avice)   (subjunctive)

<u>Catalina **sugiere** que **vayamos** al cine</u>. *Catalina suggests that we go to the cinema.*

main clause   subordinate clause

Verbs that Give Advice *Here are some verbs that give advice or indicate desires and wishes.*

aconsejar *to advise*
desear *to wish*
necesitar *to need*
pedir *to ask for*
querer *to want*
sugerir *to suggest*

PITFALL!   *If there is no change in the subject of the sentence, use the infinitive, not the subjunctive.*

No **quiero** ir a la escuela. *I don't want to go to school.*

▶ With a verb that expresses emotion

(expresses emotion)   (subjunctive)

Me <u>molesta</u> que **pienses** así. *It bothers me that you think that way.*

main clause   subordinate clause

Verbs of Emotion *Here are some verbs of emotion.*

esperar *to hope, wish*
gustar *to like*
sorprender *to surprise*
temer *to be afraid*
es triste *it's sad*
ojalá que *I hope/wish that*

Ojalá

The expression *ojalá* que is used all the time in Spanish. It means "I hope" or "I wish." You don't have to use *que* with it, but you do need to use the subjunctive.

Ojalá que pueda ir contigo.   *I hope I can go with you.*
Ojalá pueda ir contigo.   *I hope I can go with you.*

▶ With a verb that expresses doubt, denial, or disbelief

(expresses doubt)   (subjunctive)
<u>Dudan</u> que **seas** mi amigo.   *They doubt that you're my friend.*

main clause   subordinate clause

> **Verbs of Doubt, Denial, and Disbelief** *Here are some verbs of doubt, denial, and disbelief.*
>
> negar   *to deny*
> no creer   *not to believe*
> no ser cierto   *to be true [that]*
> no ser seguro   *to be certain [that]*
> ser impossible   *to be impossible [that]*

Functional Language: Constructions with Hace

To express an action that has been going on over a period of time and is still continuing at the moment of speech, use the phrase *hace* + period of time + *que* + present tense.

> (period of time)   (present tense)
> **Hace** diez años **que** vivo aquí.   *I've been living here ten years [and still do].*

▸ To ask how long something has been going on, use the phrase, *¿Cuánto tiempo hace que . . . ?* To answer the question, simply state the period of time.

> ¿Cuánto tiempo hace que usted trabaja aquí?   *How long have you been working here?*
> Cinco años.   *For five years.*

▸ To say how long ago something happened, use *hace* + period of time + *que* + preterite tense. This sentence refers to a one-time occurrence in the past.

> (period of time)   (preterite tense)
> **Hace** tres meses **que** fuimos a Perú.   *We went to Peru three months ago.*

You can also say:

> Fuimos a Perú hace tres meses.   *We went to Peru three months ago.*

Note: When *hace* does not come at the beginning of the phrase, *que* is omitted.

Sample Test Questions

PART 1, Exercise A

Turn the following adjectives into adverbs.

1. *final* _____

2. *nervioso* _____

3. *claro* _____

4. *raro* _____

5. *breve* _____

Exercise B

Write the correct adverb in the blank. Use each word in the word pool once.

tanto   por supuesto   un poco   también   acá
mucho   algo   luego   siempre   muy

1. *Estoy _____ (rather) cansada hoy.*

2. *El niño corre _____ (very) rápidamente.*

3. *_____ (of course) que voy a la escuela hoy.*

4. *Hay _____ (a little) agua en el vaso.*

5. *Tu mochila está _____ (over here).*

6. *Vamos _____ (later) al supermercado.*

7. *¡El bebé llora (cries) _____ (so much)!*

8. *Quiero ese jugo _____ (also).*

9. *Mi madre está* _____ (always) *ocupada* (busy).

10. *Me gustan* (I like) _____ (a lot) *las manzanas verdes.*

PART 2, Exercise A

Fill in the blank with the correct *se* construction. For example: "Se habla español en este negocio." Use the verb in parentheses.

1. _____ *(buscar) dos meseros* (waiters) *nuevos.*

2. _____ *(decir) que los gatos negros traen mala suerte* (bad luck).

3. _____ *(trabajar) muchas horas en la oficina.*

4. _____ *(descansar* = rest) *durante el verano.*

5. _____ *(comer) bien en la casa de Doña Fernanda.*

6. _____ *(jugar) fútbol en el parque.*

7. _____ *(dormir) bien en la cama nueva.*

8. ¡_____ *(discutir* = argue) *mucho en esta familia!*

9. _____ *(vender) pantalones y camisas.*

10. _____ *(hablar) español aquí.*

Exercise B

Fill in the blank with the correct *se* construction for unintentional actions.

1. _____ *el libro.*

    A. Se me perdieron
    B. Se me perdió

2. _____ *los anteojos* (glasses).

    A. Se nos rompieron
    B. Se nos rompió

3. _____ *la sopa en la estufa* (stove).

    A. Se les quemaron
    B. Se le quemó

4. ¡_____ *los cuadernos en casa!*

    A. Se te olvidaron
    B. Se te olvidó

5. _____ *la pelota.*

    A. Se me cayó
    B. Se me cayeron

6. _____ *la pluma.*

    A. Se os perdieron
    B. Se os perdió

Exercise C

Conjugate the following verbs in the present subjunctive mood.

1. *Yo* _____ *(estudiar).*

2. *Ellos* _____ *(comer).*

3. *Nosotros* _____ *(oír).*

4. *Tú* _____ *(dormir).*

5. *Ellas* _____ *(ganar).*

6. *Vosotros* _____ *(venir).*

7. *Yo* _____ *(haber).*

8. *Nosotras* _____ *(ser).*

9. Tú _____ (ver).

10. Vosotras _____ (estar).

Exercise D

Unscramble the following sentences. Write the complete sentence in the space provided.

1. hace | que | diez | días | en | Buenos Aires | . | estoy

   _____

2. ¿ | ? cuánto | aquí | hace que | su tío | vive | tiempo

   _____

3. seis | que | . | nos casamos | meses | hace

   _____

4. a | fueron | tres | años | . | hace | Quito

   _____

5. un | regresó | a | . | los Estados Unidos | que | hace | día

   _____

Appendix A
Vocabulary

Adjectives / los Adjetivos

An adjective must always match the gender and number of the noun it modifies. Adjectives marked with [+] usually appear before the noun.

annoying fastidioso (-a)
athletic atlético (-a)
bad malo (-a)[+]
beautiful hermoso (-a)
big grande
blond, fair-haired rubio (-a)
bored, boring aburrido (-a)
brunette, dark-haired moreno (-a)
busy ocupado (-a)
chatty, talkative hablador (-a)
cheap barato (-a)
clean limpio (-a)
closed cerrado (-a)
clumsy torpe
cool (not warm) fresco (-a)
crazy loco (-a)
cute mono (-a)
dangerous peligroso (-a)
dear querido (-a)[+]
different diferente, distinto (-a), diverso (-a)
dirty sucio (-a)
dry seco (-a)
easy fácil
empty vacío (-a)
expensive caro (-a)
famous famoso (-a)
fast rápido (-a)
fat gordo (-a)

free (no charge) gratis
free (unrestrained) libre
free (available) libre, disponible
full lleno (-a)
funny cómico (-a), humoroso (-a)
gentle tierno (-a)
good bueno (-a)[+]
handsome guapo
happy feliz
hard, difficult difícil, duro (-a)
heavy pesado (-a)
high alto (-a)
hot caliente
intelligent inteligente
interesting interesante
kind, nice amable
last último (-a)[+]
lazy perezoso (-a)
left (not right) izquierdo (-a)
light (not heavy) ligero (-a)
light (not dark) claro (-a)
long largo (-a)
loud, noisy ruidoso (-a)
mean mezquino (-a)
narrow estrecho (-a)
new nuevo (-a)
old viejo (-a)
open abierto (-a)
pleasant, agreeable simpático (-a), agradable
poor pobre
pretty bonito (-a)
proud orgulloso (-a)
quiet, peaceful tranquilo (-a)

red-haired pelirrojo (-a)
rich rico (-a)
right (not left) derecho (-a)
right (not wrong) justo (-a),
   correcto (-a)
sad triste
safe seguro (-a)
short (not long) corto (-a), breve
short (not tall) bajo (-a)
shy tímido (-a)
similar similar, semejante
silent silencioso (-a)
skinny flaco (-a)
slow lento (-a)
small pequeño (-a)

smooth suave
soft blando (-a)
strong fuerte
stupid estúpido (-a)
tall alto (-a)
thin delgado (-a)
true verdadero (-a)
ugly feo (-a)
weak débil
wet mojado (-a)
wide, broad ancho (-a)
wrong, false falso (-a),
   incorrecto (-a)
young joven

Adverb and Prepositions / los Adverbios y las Preposiciones

almost casi
maybe quizás, tal vez
only solamente, sólo
very muy

often a menudo, frecuentemente
always siempre
quickly rápidamente
slowly despacio

WHEN? HOW OFTEN?

after despúes [de]
before antes [de]
again de nuevo, otra vez
early temprano
late tarde
on time puntualmente
now ahora
still, yet todavía
not yet todavía no
already ya

never nunca, jamás
once una vez
from time to time de vez en cuando
sometimes a veces

WHERE?

far [from] lejos [de]
near, close [to] cerca [de]
next to al lado de
across from en frente de
behind detrás de
in front of delante de
between entre
above encima de
below debajo de
inside [of] dentro [de]
outside [of] afuera [de]
here aquí
there ahí
over there allí

HOW MUCH? HOW GOOD?

well bien
badly mal
better mejor
worse peor
enough bastante
not enough no bastante

too much demasiado
more más
less menos
much mucho
little poco
as... [as] tan... [como]

Animals / los Animales

farm la granja
zoo el zoo, el parque zoológico
beast la bestia
horn el cuerno
paw la pata
tail la cola
to hunt cazar

DOMESTIC ANIMALS / LOS ANIMALES DOMÉSTICOS

cat el gato
dog el perro
hen la gallina
rooster el gallo
cow la vaca
bull el toro
calf el ternero
horse el caballo
donkey el burro
sheep la oveja
ram el carnero
lamb el cordero
goat la cabra
pig el cerdo
piglet el cerdito

WILD ANIMALS / LOS ANIMALES SALVAJES

fox el zorro
wolf el lobo

deer el ciervo, el venado
lion el león
tiger el tigre
bear el oso
wild boar el jabalí
elephant el elefante
camel el camello
giraffe la jirafa
zebra la cebra
monkey el mono
mouse el ratón
rat la rata
rabbit el conejo
squirrel la ardilla
frog la rana
turtle la tortuga
lizard el lagarto, la lagartija
snake la serpiente
worm el gusano

MARINE LIFE / LA VIDA MARINA

fish el pez
shark el tiburón
whale la ballena
dolphin el delfín
jellyfish la medusa
octopus el pulpo
squid el calamar

BIRDS / LOS PÁJAROS

nest el nido
wing el ala
eagle el águila
hawk el halcón
dove, pigeon la paloma
sparrow el gorrión
crow el cuervo
parrot el loro
stork la cigüeña
owl el búho
nightingale el ruiseñor
peacock el pavo real

duck el pato
swan el cisne

INSECTS / LOS INSECTOS

ant la hormiga
bee la abeja
wasp la avispa
butterfly la mariposa
cockroach la cucaracha
fly la mosca
mosquito el mosquito
spider la araña

Around Town / por la Ciudad

address la dirección
street la calle
town center el centro

PUBLIC INSTITUTIONS / LAS INSTITUCIONES PÚBLICAS

post office la oficina de correos
mail el correo
letter la carta
to send enviar
stamp el sello
town hall el ayuntamiento
hospital el hospital
church la iglesia
library la biblioteca
pool la piscina
stadium el estadio
park el parque

MONEY / EL DINERO

How much does it cost? ¿Cuánto cuesta?
to buy comprar
to sell vender
price el precio

to pay pagar
in cash en efectivo
by check con cheque
by credit card con tarjeta de crédito
receipt el recibo
change (from a purchase) el cambio
cash register la caja
bank el banco
ATM el cajero automático

SHOPPING / LAS COMPRAS

to run errands, to go shopping ir de compras
market el mercado
mall el centro comercial
store la tienda
department store el almacén
sale las rebajas
bakery la panadería
bookstore la librería
butcher shop la carnicería
grocery store la tienda de comestibles
supermarket el supermercado
laundromat la lavandería

Calendar / el Calendario

DATES / LAS FECHAS

What is today's date? ¿Cuál es la
fecha de hoy?

It is... Es...

May 1st el primero de mayo

March 2nd el dos de marzo

October 31st el treinta y uno de
octubre

today hoy

yesterday ayer

tomorrow mañana

day before yesterday anteayer

day after tomorrow pasado
mañana

DAYS OF THE WEEK / LOS DÍAS DE LA SEMANA

Monday lunes

Tuesday martes

Wednesday miércoles

Thursday jueves

Friday viernes

Saturday sábado

Sunday domingo

What day of the week is it? ¿Qué
día es?

It's Monday. Es lunes.

MONTHS / LOS MESES

January enero

February febrero

March marzo

April abril

May mayo

June junio

July julio

August agosto

September septiembre

October octubre

SEASONS / LAS ESTACIONES

winter el invierno

summer el verano

spring la primavera

autumn el otoño

MEASURING TIME

week la semana

last week la semana pasada

next week la semana próxima

in a week en una semana

in two weeks en dos semanas

weekly semanal

weekend el fin de semana

month el mes

year el año

three years ago hace tres años

last year el año pasado

decade la década

in the fifties durante los años
cincuenta

century el siglo

HOLIDAYS / LOS DÍAS FERIADOS

Christmas la Navidad

Christmas Eve la Nochebuena

New Year's Day el Día del Año
Nuevo

Holy Week la Semana Santa

Easter la Pascua

Clothing / la Ropa

to wear, carry llevar
to put on ponerse
to take off quitarse
to get dressed vestirse
to get undressed desnudarse
This skirt fits you well. Esta falda
  te queda bien.

SEWING / LA COSTURA

to sew coser
thread el hilo
needle la aguja
scissors las tijeras
to iron planchar
to clean limpiar

GARMENTS / LAS PRENDAS

sleeve la manga
pocket el bolsillo
long largo (-a)
short corto (-a)
loose flojo (-a)
tight apretado (-a)
lace el encaje
silk la seda
cotton el algodón
fur la piel
leather el cuero
checked a cuadros
polka-dotted con lunares
striped a rayas
fashionable de moda

UNDERGARMENTS / LA ROPA INTERIOR

bra el sostén
(men's) briefs los calzoncillos
(women's) underpants las bragas
half-slip la enagua corta

slip la combinación
tights las medias

EVERYDAY CLOTHES / LA ROPA DIARIA

shirt la camisa
sweater el suéter
T-shirt la camiseta
pants los pantalones
belt el cinturón
jeans los vaqueros
shorts los pantalones cortos

suit el traje
suit jacket la chaqueta deportiva
tuxedo el esmoquin
tie la corbata
vest, waistcoat el chaleco
suspenders los tirantes

blouse la blusa
skirt la falda
dress el vestido
suit el traje
stockings las medias

OUTERWEAR / LA ROPA EXTERIOR

coat el abrigo
jacket la chaqueta
raincoat el impermeable
hat el sombrero
(knit) hat el gorro
scarf la bufanda
shawl el chal
gloves los guantes

pajamas la pijama
swimsuit el traje de baño

FOOTWEAR / EL CALZADO

shoes los zapatos
high heels los tacones altos
sneakers los zapatos para deporte
slippers las pantuflas
boots las botas
socks los calcetines

ACCESSORIES / LOS ACCESORIOS

bag la bolsa
handbag el bolso
backpack la mochila
wallet la cartera
glasses las gafas
sunglasses las gafas de sol
umbrella el paraguas

JEWELRY / LAS JOYAS

silver la plata
gold el oro
copper el cobre
platinum el platino
diamond el diamante
emerald la esmeralda
ruby el rubí
sapphire el zafiro
pearl la perla
bracelet la pulsera
brooch el broche
earrings los aretes, los pendientes
ring el anillo
nosering el aro para la nariz
wedding ring la alianza
necklace el collar
watch el reloj

Colors / los Colores

white blanco (-a)
yellow amarillo (-a)
pink rosado (-a)
red rojo (-a)
orange anaranjado (-a)
green verde
blue azul
purple morado (-a)

brown marrón
gray gris
black negro (-a)

gold dorado (-a)
silver plateado (-a)

light blue azul claro
dark blue azul oscuro

Directions / las Direcciones

north el norte
south el sur
east el este
west el oeste
northeast el noreste
northwest el noroeste
southeast el sureste

southwest el suroeste

left a la izquierda
right a la derecha
straight ahead derecho
Turn right. Doble a la derecha.

...in the right direction ...en el sentido correcto

...in the wrong direction ...en el sentido contrario

Education / la Educación

to learn aprender
to study estudiar
to know saber
to teach enseñar

SCHOOL / LA ESCUELA

nursery school el parvulario
elementary school la escuela primaria
junior high school la escuela intermedia
high school la escuela secundaria
college, university la universidad
grade (level) el nivel
grade (mark) la nota
class (group) la clase
class (lesson) la lección
recess el descanso
cafeteria la cafetería

pupil, student el alumno, el estudiante
university student el estudiante universitario
teacher, professor el profesor, la profesora
elementary school teacher el maestro, la maestra

SCHOOL YEAR / EL AÑO ESCOLAR

vacation las vacaciones
summer vacation las vacaciones de verano
day off el día libre

first day of school el primer día de la escuela

SUBJECTS / LAS MATERIAS

reading la lectura
writing la escritura
spelling la ortografía
mathematics las matemáticas
art el arte
fine arts las bellas artes
music la música
drama el teatro
geography la geografía
history la historia
science la ciencia
biology la biología
chemistry la química
physics la física
computer science la informática
political science las ciencias políticas
economics la economía
philosophy la filosofía
psychology la psicología
literature la literatura
foreign language el idioma extranjero
English el inglés
French el francés
Spanish el español
Italian el italiano
German el alemán

SCHOOL SUPPLIES / EL MATERIAL ESCOLAR

binder la carpeta
notebook el cuaderno
workbook el libro de ejercicios
book el libro
glue la pega
paper el papel
sheet (of paper) la hoja de papel
pen el bolígrafo
pencil el lápiz
stapler la grapadora
chalk la tiza

IN THE CLASSROOM / EN EL AULA

question la pregunta
to raise (one's) hand levantar la mano
answer la respuesta
exercise el ejercicio
essay la composición, el ensayo
homework la tarea
to do homework hacer la tarea
test el examen
to take a... tomar un...

to pass a... aprobar un...
to fail a... suspender un...
chalkboard la pizarra
to erase borrar
desk (pupil's) el pupitre
desk (teacher's) el escritorio

UNIVERSITY / LA UNIVERSIDAD

department el departamento
school (division) la facultad
faculty el profesorado
medical school la facultad de medecina
law school la facultad de derecho
diploma el diploma
to have a diploma in... tener título en...
degree el título
bachelor of arts (B.A.) el licenciado en Letras
bachelor of science (B.S.) el licenciado en Ciencias
master's degree la maestría
doctorate (Ph.D.) el doctorado

Encounters / los Encuentros

PLEASANTRIES

please por favor
thank you gracias
thank you very much muchas gracias
You're welcome. De nada.
No problem. No hay de que.
Welcome to... Bienvendos a...

HELLO AND GOOD-BYE

Good morning Buenos días
Good afternoon Buenas tardes
Good evening Buenas noches
Hello Hola
Good-bye Adiós
See you soon. Hasta pronto.
See you later. Hasta luego.
See you tomorrow. Hasta mañana.
Until next time. Hasta la próxima.

Have a nice day. Que pase buen día.

HOW DO YOU DO?

How are you doing? ¿Cómo está
usted? / ¿Cómo estás? (*fam.*)

I'm... Estoy...
   [very] well [muy] bien
   [very] bad [muy] mal
   so-so así así

How's it going? ¿Qué tal?
Fine. Bien.
It's going well. Va bien.
   ...badly. ...mal.
Not bad Más o menos.

What's new? ¿Qué hay de nuevo?
Nothing much. No mucho.

yes sí
no no
maybe quizás

INTRODUCTIONS

What's your name? ¿Cómo se
llama? / ¿Cómo te llamas? (*fam.*)
My name is... Me llamo...
Pleased to meet you. Encantado
(-a).
I'd like you to meet... Querría
presentarle a...
This is... Le presento a...

Where are you from? ¿De dónde es
usted? / ¿De dónde eres? (*fam.*)
I'm from... Soy de...

first name el nombre
last name el apellido

Miss señorita (Srta.)
Mr./Sir señor (Sr.)
Mrs./Ma'am señora (Sra.)

Food / la Comida

to eat comer
to drink beber
to be hungry tener hambre
to be thirsty tener sed
to cook cocinar
to heat calentar
to taste probar

MEALS / LAS COMIDAS

breakfast el desayuno
lunch el almuerzo
dinner, supper la cena
snack la merienda

PREPARATION / LA PREPARACIÓN

raw crudo (-a)
fresh fresco (-a)
cooked cocido (-a)
baked cocido (-a) al horno
fried frito (-a)
steamed cocido (-a) al vapor
roasted asado (-a)
grilled asado (-a) a la parrilla

TASTE / EL SABOR

bitter amargo (-a)
sour agrio (-a)
sweet dulce

salty   salado (-a)
spicy   picante
tasty, delicious   rico (-a),
   delicioso (-a)

DAIRY PRODUCTS / LOS PRODUCTOS LÁCTEOS

milk   la leche
skim...   ...desnatada
2-percent...   ...semidesnatada
butter   la mantequilla
cheese   el queso
cream   la crema
sour cream   la crema agria
yogurt   el yogur

GRAINS / LOS CEREALES

cereal   el cereal
bread   el pan
whole wheat   ...integral
rye   ...de centeno
rice   el arroz

CONDIMENTS / LOS CONDIMENTOS

sauce   la salsa
spice   la especia
vinegar   el vinagre
salt   la sal
sugar   el azúcar
pepper (spice)   la pimienta
saffron   el azafrán
garlic   el ajo
[olive] oil   el aceite [de oliva]
mayonnaise   la mayonesa
mustard   la mostaza
jam   la mermelada

DESSERTS / LOS POSTRES

cake   la torta
ice cream   el helado
cookie   la galleta
whipped cream   la nata montada
chocolate   el chocolate
caramel custard   el flan

LIGHT MEALS / LA COMIDA LIGERA

egg   el huevo
salad   la ensalada
dressing   el aderezo
sandwich   el sandwich
cold cuts (deli)   los embutidos

MEAT / LA CARNE

beef   la carne (de res, de vaca)
chop   la chuleta
ham   el jamón
lamb   (la carne de) cordero
liver   el hígado
loin   el lomo
pork   (la carne de) cerdo
sausage   la salchicha, el chorizo
veal   la ternera
venison   el venado

FISH AND SEAFOOD / EL PESCADO Y LOS MARISCOS

lobster   la langosta
crab   el cangrejo
shrimp   el camarón
shellfish   los mariscos
mussels   los mejillones
clams   las almejas
fish   el pescado
filet   el filete
tuna(fish)   el atún
salmon   el salmón

sole   el lenguado
trout   la trucha

POULTRY / LA CARNE DE AVES DE CORRAL

chicken   el pollo
turkey   el pavo
duck   el pato
breast   la pechuga

FRUIT / LAS FRUTAS

dried fruit   los frutos secos
apple   la manzana
banana   el plátano
grape   la uva
raisin   la pasa
grapefruit   la toronja
lemon   el limón
melon   el melón
orange   la naranja
peach   el melocotón
pear   la pera
plum   la ciruela
pineapple   la piña
watermelon   la sandía

BERRIES / LAS BAYAS

blueberry   el arándano
cherry   la cereza
raspberry   la frambuesa
strawberry   la fresa

VEGETABLES / LAS VERDURAS

potato   la patata
tomato   el tomate
cucumber   el pepino
pepper (vegetable)   el pimiento
onion   la cebolla
leek   el puerro

carrot   la zanahoria
lettuce   la lechuga
cabbage   la col
cauliflower   la coliflor
spinach   la espinaca
beans   los frijoles
[green] beans   la judía [verde]
peas   los guisantes
corn   el maíz
eggplant   la berenjena
mushroom   el champiñón
asparagus   el espárrago
nut, walnut   la nuez
hazelnut   la avellana
peanut   el cacahuete

BEVERAGES / LAS BEBIDAS

coffee   el café
tea   el té
with milk   con leche
herbal tea   la infusión
hot chocolate   el chocolate
juice   el jugo
orange juice   el jugo de naranja
Coke   la Coca-Cola
milk   la leche
water   el agua
ice   el hielo

ALCOHOL / EL ALCOHOL

wine   el vino
hard cider   la sidra
dry   seco (-a)
sweet   dulce
beer   la cerveza
drunk   borracho (-a)

UTENSILS / LOS UTENSILIOS

knife   el cuchillo
fork   el tenedor
spoon   la cuchara

plate   el plato
bowl   el bol, el cuenco
cup   la taza
cup of tea   una taza de té
glass   el vaso
napkin   la servilleta

frying pan   el sartén
bottle opener   el abrebotellas
corkscrew   el sacacorchos
coffee pot   la cafetera
can opener   el abrelatas

Geography / la Geografía

map   el mapa, la carta
country   el país
city   la ciudad
countryside   el campo, el paisaje
island   la isla

BODIES OF WATER / LAS MASAS DE AGUA

ocean   el océano
sea   el mar
lake   el lago
river   el río
stream   el arroyo
marsh, swamp   el pantano

LANDSCAPE / EL PAISAJE

mountain   la montaña
rock (boulder)   el peñasco
hill   la colina
valley   el valle
field   el campo
forest   el bosque
flower   la flor
tree   el árbol
desert   el desierto

CONTINENTS / LOS CONTINENTES

Africa   África
America   América
   (North)   Norteamérica
   (South)   Sudamérica
Asia   Asia
Australia   Australia
Europe   Europa

COUNTRIES / LOS PAÍSES

Argentina   la Argentina
Brazil   el Brasil
Canada   el Canadá
China   la China
Egypt   Egipto
England   Inglaterra
France   Francia
Germany   Alemania
Greece   Grecia
India   la India
Ireland   Irlanda
Israel   Israel
Italy   Italia
Japan   el Japón
Korea   Corea
Mexico   México
Morocco   Marruecos
Netherlands   los Países Bajos
Peru   el Perú
Portugal   Portugal

Philippines las Filipinas
Russia Rusia
Scotland Escocia
Spain España
Switzerland Suiza

Thailand Tailandia
Tunisia Túnez
United Kingdom el Reino Unido
United States los Estados Unidos

Health / la Salud

How are you feeling? ¿Cómo se siente?
I don't feel well. No me siento bien.
I feel... Me siento...
   ...well. ...bien.
   ...better. ...mejor.
   ...worse. ...peor.
It hurts. Me duele.
I feel nauseated. Tengo náuseas.
I have... Me duele...
   ...a headache. ...la cabeza.
   ...a sore throat. ...la garganta.
   ...a stomachache. ...el estómago.
I have... Me duelen...
   ...a toothache. ...los dientes.
   ...an earache. ...los oídos.
   ...a backache. ...la espalda.
I have a cold. Tengo resfriado.

to be hot tener calor
to be cold tener frío
to be allergic [to] tener alergia [a]
to break romperse
   ...an arm ...el brazo
to sneeze estornudar
to cough toser
to faint desmayarse
sick enfermo (-a)
healthy, fit sano (-a)
tired cansado (-a)
weak débil
blind ciego (-a)
deaf sordo (-a)

disease, illness la enfermedad
pain el dolor
cough la tos
cold el resfriado
fever la fiebre
flu la gripe
chicken pox la varicela
broken [arm] [el brazo] roto
bruise la contusión
wound la herida
scar la cicatriz
AIDS el SIDA
HIV-positive seropositivo (-a)
heart attack el infarto

doctor el médico
nurse el enfermero
height la altura
weight el peso
pulse el pulso
blood pressure la tensión arterial
medicine (drug) la medicina
bandage el vendaje
Band-Aid la tirita
a pill una píldora
the Pill la píldora anticonceptiva
drops las gotas
therapy la terapia
wheelchair la silla de ruedas

diet la dieta
to lose weight, get thinner adelgazar
to gain weight, get fatter engordar
to fast ayunar

HYGIENE AND GROOMING / LA HIGIENE PERSONAL

soap   el jabón
razor   el rastrillo
shampoo   el champú
toothpaste   la pasta de dientes
toothbrush   el cepillo de dientes
comb   el peine
hairbrush   el cepillo
makeup   el maquillaje
lipstick   el lápiz de labios
pimple   el grano
blackhead   la espinilla

to wash (self)   lavar(se)
to wash (one's) hands   lavarse las manos
to bathe   bañarse
to shower   ducharse
to shave   afeitarse
to brush (one's) teeth   cepillarse los dientes
to brush (one's) hair   cepillarse el cabello
to comb (self)   peinar(se)
to put on makeup   maquillarse

Household / el Hogar

HOUSE / LA CASA

apartment   el apartamento
apartment building   el edificio de apartamentos
subsidized housing   la vivienda subvencionada
yard, garden   el jardín
lawn   el césped, el patio
garage   el garaje
roof   el techo
wall   la pared
floor   el piso
ceiling   el techo
window   la ventana
balcony   el balcón
floor (level)   la planta
ground fl.   la planta baja
second fl.   la primera planta
attic   el desván
basement   el sótano
stairs   la escalera
elevator   el ascensor
door   la puerta

bell   el timbre
key   la llave

ROOMS AND FURNISHINGS / LOS CUARTOS Y LOS MUEBLES

furniture   los muebles
living room   la sala
couch   el sofá
armchair   el sillón
TV (set)   el televisor
to watch TV   mirar la televisión
shelf   el estante
curtain   la cortina
rug   la alfombra
clock   el reloj
dining room   el comedor
table   la mesa
chair   la silla
bedroom   el cuarto, el dormitorio, la habitación
bed   la cama
   mattress   el colchón
   sheet   la sábana

blanket   la manta
pillow   la almohada
dresser   la cómoda
  drawer   el cajón
  mirror   el espejo
closet   el armario
bathroom   el cuarto de baño, el baño
bathtub   la bañera
shower   la ducha
toilet   el inodoro
sink   el lavabo
towel   la toalla
kitchen   la cocina
refrigerator   la nevera,
  el refrigerador

oven   el horno
microwave   el microondas
dishwasher   el lavaplatos
stool   el taburete
vacuum   la aspiradora

TELEPHONE / EL TELÉFONO

phone call   la llamada telefónica
phone number   el número de
  teléfono
to pick up   descolgar
to dial   marcar
to hang up   colgar
cell phone   el teléfono celular

Leisure / el Ocio

entertainment   la diversión
hobby   el pasatiempo

museum   el museo
exhibition   la exposición
show   el espectáculo
performance   la representación
concert   el concierto
movie theater   el cine
movie   la película
theater   el teatro
play   la obra
opera   la ópera
circus   el circo

bar, pub   el bar
club   el club
nightclub   la discoteca
to go clubbing   ir de discotecas
party   la fiesta

MUSIC / LA MÚSICA

to play...   tocar...
the flute   la flauta
the guitar   la guitarra
the piano   el piano
the violin   el violín

SPORTS / LOS DEPORTES

to play sports   practicar, jugar
  deportes
to play tennis   jugar al tenis
game/match   el partido
baseball   el béisbol
basketball   el baloncesto,
  el básquetbol
dancing   el baile
fencing   la esgrima
football   el fútbol americano
hockey   el hockey
to go horse-back riding   montar a
  caballo
ice skating   el patinaje sobre hielo

to skate   patinar
sailing   la vela
ski   el esquí
soccer   el fútbol
swimming   la natación
to swim   nadar
tennis   el tenis

GAMES / LOS JUEGOS

to play...   jugar...
   cards   a las cartas
   checkers   a las damas
   chess   al ajedrez
   pool   al billar
   round, hand   la vuelta
   video game   el videojuego

On the Road / en el Camino

to drive   conducir, manejar
driver's license   la licencia de manejar
driver   el conductor
passenger   el pasajero
to get into (a vehicle)   subir a[l vehículo]
to get out of (a vehicle)   bajar de[l vehículo]
pedestrian   el peatón

CAR / EL COCHE

windshield   el parabrisas
wheel (of car)   la llanta
tire   el neumático
steering wheel   el volante
seatbelt   el cinturón de seguridad
headlight   la luz delantera
turn signal   la direccional
windshield wiper   el limpiaparabrisas

gasoline   la gasolina
gas station   la estación de servicio
engine   el motor
oil   el aceite
brake   el freno
breakdown   la avería
to be broken, not working   estar estropeado

ROAD / EL CAMINO

traffic   el tráfico
lane   el carril
intersection   la intersección
(traffic) light   el semáforo
street   la calle
highway   la autopista
rotary   la glorieta
road map   el mapa de carteras
to park   estacionar, aparcar
parking lot/spot   el estacionamiento

Relationships / las Relaciones

FAMILY / LA FAMILIA

parents   los padres
relatives   los parientes
mother   la madre
mom   la mamá
father   el padre
dad   el papá
husband   el marido
wife   la mujer
spouse   el esposo, la esposa
son   el hijo
daughter   la hija
brother   el hermano
sister   la hermana
only child   el hijo único
younger   menor
older   mayor
twin   el gemelo

aunt   la tía
uncle   el tío
nephew   el sobrino
niece   la sobrina
cousin   el primo, la prima

grandparents   los abuelos
grandfather   el abuelo
grandmother   la abuela
great-grandfather   el bisabuelo
grandchildren   los nietos
grandson   el nieto
granddaughter   la nieta
great-granddaughter   la bisnieta

father-in-law   el suegro
mother-in-law   la suegra
son-in-law   el yerno
daughter-in-law   la nuera
brother-in-law   el cuñado
sister-in-law   la cuñada

stepfather   el padrastro
stepmother   la madrastra
stepson   el hijastro
stepdaughter   la hijastra
stepbrother   el hermanastro
stepsister   la hermanastra
half-brother   el medio hermano
half-sister   la media hermana

FRIENDS / LOS AMIGOS

friend   el amigo, la amiga
best friend   el mejor amigo, la mejor amiga
buddy, pal   el amigote
acquaintance   el conocido, la conocida

boy/girlfriend   el novio, la novia
my boyfriend   mi novio
my girlfriend   mi novia
my friend   mi amigo/a
lover   el amante (m, f)
hetero-/homosexual   hétero-/homosexual

godfather   el padrino
godmother   la madrina
godson   el ahijado
goddaughter   la ahijada

CYCLE OF LIFE / EL CICLO DE LA VIDA

birth   el nacimiento
to be born   nacer
baby   el bebé
boy   el chico
girl   la chica
child   el niño, la niña

to grow up crecer
young people los jóvenes
man el hombre
woman la mujer
single soltero (-a)
to be dating salir juntos
to sleep together dormir juntos
to get engaged comprometerse

engagement el compromiso
to get married casarse
wedding la boda
reception la recepción
maiden name el apellido de soltera
honeymoon la luna de miel
pregnant embarazada

divorce el divorcio
death la muerte
to die morir
widow la viuda
widower el viudo
mourning el luto
orphan el huérfano, la huérfana

EMOTIONS / LAS EMOCIONES

love el amor
hate el odio
friendship la amistad
respect el respeto, la consideración

Restaurant / el Restaurante

What would you like? ¿Qué querría?
I'll have... Quiero...
Where is the restroom? ¿Dónde están los servicios?
I'm [too] full. Estoy [demasiado] lleno.
menu el menú
tip included servicio incluido
waiter/waitress el camarero/la camarera
place setting el cubierto
water pitcher una jarra de agua
empty vacío (-a)
full (not empty) lleno (-a)
to sit down sentarse

to order pedir
to share compartir
eat-in para tomar
take-out para llevar
to pay pagar
check, bill la cuenta
tip la propina

COURSES / LOS PLATOS

drinks las bebidas
appetizer, starter el aperitivo
first course el primer plato
main course, entrée el plato principal
dessert el postre

Time / la Hora

CLOCK TIME

What time is it? ¿Qué hora es?
Do you have the time? / Do you
know what time it is? ¿Tiene la
hora?
What time is the concert? ¿A qué
hora es el concierto?

When using the 24-hour clock, do not
indicate *a.m.* and *p.m.* (with
expressions such as *de la mañana*, etc.)
or use special terms for the half- and
quarter-hour (*y cuarto*, etc.).

- 15:30 (*3:30 p.m.*) reads *quince horas*
  y treinta minutos.
- Son las 22:45 (*It is 10:45 p.m.*)
  reads *Son las* veintidós horas y
  cuarenta y cinco minútos.

It is... Es...
  noon mediodía
  midnight medianoche
  1:00 la una
  1:30 la una y media
It is... Son...
  2:00 las dos

  2:10 las dos y diez
  2:15 las dos y cuarto
  2:30 las dos y media
  2:45 las tres menos cuarto
  2:50 las tres menos diez
at night de la noche
in the morning de la mañana
in the afternoon/evening de la
  tarde

TIME OF DAY

morning la mañana
  dawn el alba
   sunrise el amanecer, la salida
    del sol
day el día
  afternoon la tarde
evening la tarde
  dusk el crepúsculo
   sunset el anochecer, la puesta
    del sol
night la noche
hour la hora
minute el minuto
second el segundo

Travel / Viajar

vacation las vacaciones
to go on vacation ir de vacaciones
business travel el viaje de negocios
trip el viaje
to visit visitar
luggage el equipaje
suitcase la maleta
to pack hacer la maleta

hotel el hotel
stay la estancia
information la información
passport el pasaporte
visa el visado
customs la aduana
(city) map la mapa, el plano

BUS / EL AUTOBÚS

bus driver el chófer de autobús
bus station la estación de autobuses
passenger el pasajero
[bus] stop la parada
seat el asiento

TRAIN / EL TREN

station la estación de tren
ticket window la taquilla
timetable el horario
ticket el billete, el boleto
one-way ...de ida
round-trip ...de ida y vuelta
(ticket) price la tarifa
to validate (a ticket) validar
platform la plataforma
track la vía
exit la salida
arrival la llegada

departure la salida
delay el retraso
sleeper place la litera
connection la correspondencia

PLANE / EL AVIÓN

airport el aeropuerto
flight el vuelo
takeoff el despegue
landing el aterrizaje
gate la puerta

OTHER VEHICLES / OTROS VEHÍCULOS

boat el barco
bike, bicycle la bicicleta
motorcycle la motocicleta
subway el metro
token la ficha
taxi el taxi

Weather / el Tiempo

How is the weather? ¿Qué tiempo hace?
What is the temperature? ¿A qué está la temperatura?
It is 20 degrees... Está a 20 grados...
  below zero. bajo cero.
It is... Hace...
  nice buen tiempo
  hot calor
  cool fresco
  cold frío
  bad mal tiempo
It's raining. Llueve.
It's snowing. Nieva.
It's hailing. Graniza.
It's sunny. Hace sol.

It's windy. Hace viento.
It's cloudy. Está nublado.

air el aire
cloud la nube
fog la niebla
frost la helada
hail el granizo
lightning el relámpago
lightning bolt el rayo
sun el sol
moon la luna
rain la lluvia
snow la nieve
wind el viento
rainbow el arco iris
shade la sombra

sky   el cielo
star   la estrella
storm   la tormenta

thunder   el trueno
humidity   la humedad
forecast   el pronóstico

Work / el Trabajo

to work   trabajar
job (trade)   el oficio
job (employment)   el trabajo, el empleo
job (task)   la tarea
to apply for [a job]   solicitar [un trabajo]
job interview   la entrevista
application (form)   la solicitud
unemployed   desempleado (-a)
retired   jubilado (-a)
(trade) union   el sindicato
strike   la huelga
to strike   declararse en huelga
to earn   ganar
wages, salary   el sueldo
taxes   los impuestos
boss   el jefe
company   la compañía, la empresa
office   la oficina
meeting   la reunión
to intern   internar
factory   la fábrica

OCCUPATIONS / LAS PROFESIONES

He/she is a lawyer.   Es abogado (-a).
He/she is an engineer.   Es ingeniero (-a).

To indicate a person's profession, do not use an article when using the verb "to be": *Soy panadero.* But: *Hablo con el panadero.*

accountant   contador (-a)
actor   actor (-triz)
artist   artista (m, f)
baker   panadero (-a)
businessman/woman   hombre/ mujer de negocios
civil servant   funcionario (-a)
computer specialist   informático (-a)
cook   cocinero (-a)
dancer   bailerín (-a)
dentist   dentista (m, f)
doctor   doctor (-a), médico (-a)
driver   conductor (-a)
truck driver   camionero (-a)
editor   editor (-a), redactor (-a)
engineer   ingeniero (-a)
farmer   granjero (-a)
fireman   bombero (-a)
hairdresser   peluquero (-a)
journalist   periodista (m, f)
lawyer   abogado (-a)
librarian   bibliotecario (-a)
mailman   cartero (-a)
musician   músico (-a)
nurse   enfermero (-a)
pilot   piloto (-a)
photographer   fotógrafo (-a)
plumber   fontanero (-a)
policeman   policía, mujer policía
salesperson   dependiente (m, f), vendedor (-a)
secretary   secretario (-a)
security guard   guardia (m, f)
singer   cantante (m, f)

student estudiante (m, f)
soldier soldado (-a)
teacher profesor (-a)

worker (factory) obrero (-a)
writer escritor (-a)

Verbs / los Verbos

Verbs with irregular conjugations or spelling changes are marked with [+].

to allow permitir
to answer responder
to arrive llegar[+]
to ask preguntar
to ask for pedir[+]
to attend asistir
to be ser[+], estar[+]
to be able to poder[+]
to become haverse[+], ponerse[+], llegar[+] a ser, convertirse[+] en
to begin comenzar[+], empezar[+]
to believe creer[+]
to borrow pedir[+] prestado
to be born nacer[+]
to bring (somebody) llevar
to bring (something) traer[+]
to build construir[+]
to choose escoger[+]
to climb, go up montar
to close cerrar[+]
to come venir[+]
to come back volver[+]
to cry llorar
to descend, go down bajar
to discuss discutir
to do hacer[+]
to drive conducir[+]
to enter entrar
to fall caerse[+]
to fear temer
to feel sentirse[+]
to finish terminar

to follow seguir[+]
to forget olvidar
to have fun divertirse[+]
to hope esperar
to get up levantarse
to give dar[+]
to go ir[+]
to go to bed acostarse[+]
to hate odiar
to have to, owe deber
to hear oír[+]
to help ayudar
to know (fact, skill) saber[+]
to know (person, place) conocer[+]
to laugh reírse[+]
to leave salir[+]
to lend prestar
to lie mentir[+]
to listen escuchar
to live (exist) vivir
to live (dwell in) habitar
to look at mirar
to look for buscar[+]
to lose perder[+]
to love amar
to miss (train) perder[+]
to obey obedecer[+]
to open abrir
to pass [by something] pasar [por algo]
to play (instrument) tocar[+]
to play (sport) jugar[+]
to prefer preferir[+]
to promise prometer
to put poner[+], meter

to read leer[+]

to realize [something] darse[+]
cuenta [de algo]

to receive recibir[+]

to remember [something]
acordarse[+] [de algo]

to remind recordar[+]

to return (to a place) volver[+]

to return [something] devolver[+]
[algo]

to run correr

to say, tell decir[+]

to see ver[+]

to seem, appear parecer[+]

to show mostrar[+]

to shut up, be quiet callarse

to sing cantar

to sit down sentarse[+]

to sleep dormir[+]

to fall asleep dormirse[+]

to smell oler[+]

to smile sonreírse[+]

to speak, talk hablar

to stay, remain quedarse

to take tomar

to take (along, away) llevar

to tell [a story] contar[+] [una
historia]

to think [about something] pensar[+]
[en algo]

to throw (away) tirar

to understand comprender,
entender[+]

to wake up despertarse[+]

to walk caminar, andar[+]

to watch mirar

to wish, want querer[+]

to worry [about something]
preocuparse [por algo]

to write escribir[+]

Appendix B
Verb Charts

On the following pages are charts for all the verbs you've seen in this book, along with some others that you will encounter in your studies.

We've left out the subject pronouns. As you'll remember from your lessons, the subject pronouns aren't always necessary. Context and verb endings should help you to identify the subject of the verbs.

To refresh your memory, here are the subject pronouns.

Person	Singular	Plural
1st	yo	nosotros nosotras
2nd	tú	vosotros vosotras
3rd	él ella usted	ellos ellas ustedes

A

abrir   (to open)

Present		Preterite	
abro	abrimos	abrí	abrimos
abres	abrís	abriste	abristeis
abre	abren	abrió	abrieron

Imperfect		Present Subjunctive	
abría	abríamos	abra	abramos
abrías	abríais	abras	abráis
abría	abrían	abra	abran

actuar   (to act, to behave)

Present		Preterite	
actúo	actuamos	actué	actuamos
actúas	actuáis	actuaste	actuasteis
actúa	actúan	actuó	actuaron

Imperfect		Present Subjunctive	
actuaba	actuábamos	actúe	actuemos
actuabas	actuabais	actúes	actuéis
actuaba	actuaban	actúe	actúen

almorzar   (to have lunch)

Present		Preterite	
almuerzo	almorzamos	almorcé	almorzamos
almuerzas	almorzáis	almorzaste	almorzasteis
almuerza	almuerzan	almorzó	almorzaron

Imperfect		Present Subjunctive	
almorzaba	almorzábamos	almuerce	almorcemos
almorzabas	almorzabais	almuerces	almorcéis
almorzaba	almorzaban	almuerce	almuercen

andar (to walk, to go)

Present		Preterite	
ando	andamos	anduve	anduvimos
andas	andáis	anduviste	anduvisteis
anda	andan	anduvo	anduvieron

Imperfect		Present Subjunctive	
andaba	andábamos	ande	andemos
andabas	andabais	andes	andéis
andaba	andaban	ande	anden

aprender (to learn)

Present		Preterite	
aprendo	aprendemos	aprendí	aprendimos
aprendes	aprendéis	aprendiste	aprendisteis
aprende	aprenden	aprendió	aprendieron

Imperfect		Present Subjunctive	
aprendía	aprendíamos	aprenda	aprendamos
aprendías	aprendíais	aprendas	aprendáis
aprendía	aprendían	aprenda	aprendan

B

buscar (to search for, to look for)

Present		Preterite	
busco	buscamos	busqué	buscamos
buscas	buscáis	buscaste	buscasteis
busca	buscan	buscó	buscan

Imperfect		Present Subjunctive	
buscaba	buscábamos	busque	busquemos
buscabas	buscabais	busques	busquéis
buscaba	buscaban	busque	busquen

C

caer (to fall)

Present		Preterite	
caigo	caemos	caí	caímos
caes	caéis	caíste	caísteis
cae	caen	cayó	cayeron

Imperfect		Present Subjunctive	
caía	caíamos	caiga	caigamos
caías	caíais	caigas	caigáis
caía	caían	caiga	caigan

cantar (to sing)

Present		Preterite	
canto	cantamos	canté	cantamos
cantas	cantáis	cantaste	cantasteis
canta	cantan	cantó	cantaron

Imperfect		Present Subjunctive	
cantaba	cantábamos	cante	cantemos
cantabas	cantabais	cantes	cantéis
cantaba	cantaban	cante	canten

cerrar (to close)

Present		Preterite	
cierro	cerramos	cerré	cerramos
cierras	cerráis	cerraste	cerrasteis
cierra	cierran	cerró	cerraron

Imperfect		Present Subjunctive	
cerraba	cerrábamos	cierre	cerremos
cerrabas	cerrabais	cierres	cerréis
cerraba	cerraban	cierre	cierren

comer (to eat)

Present		Preterite	
como	comemos	comí	comimos
comes	coméis	comiste	comisteis
come	comen	comió	comieron

Imperfect		Present Subjunctive	
comía	comíamos	como	comamos
comías	comíais	comas	comáis
comía	comían	coma	coman

componer (to fix, to repair)

Present		Preterite	
compongo	componemos	compuse	compusimos
compones	componéis	compusiste	compusisteis
compone	componen	compuso	compusieron

Imperfect		Present Subjunctive	
componía	componíamos	componga	compongamos
componías	componíais	compongas	compongáis
componía	componían	componga	compongan

comprender (to understand, to comprehend)

Present		Preterite	
comprendo	comprendemos	comprendí	comprendimos
comprendes	comprendéis	comprendiste	comprendisteis
comprende	comprenden	comprendió	comprendieron

Imperfect		Present Subjunctive	
comprendía	comprendíamos	comprenda	comprendamos
comprendías	comprendíais	comprendas	comprendáis
comprendía	comprendían	comprenda	comprendan

conducir (to drive)

Present		Preterite	
conduzco	conducimos	conduje	condujimos
conduces	conducís	condujiste	condujisteis
conduce	conducen	condujo	condujeron

Imperfect		Present Subjunctive	
conducía	conducíamos	conduzca	conduzcamos
conducías	conducíais	conduzcas	conduzcáis
conducía	conducían	conduzca	conduzcan

confiar (to confide, to trust)

Present		Preterite	
confío	confiamos	confié	confiamos
confías	confiáis	confiaste	confiasteis
confía	confían	confió	confiaron

Imperfect		Present Subjunctive	
confiaba	confiábamos	confíe	confiemos
confiabas	confiabais	confíes	confiéis
confiaba	confiaban	confíe	confíen

conocer (to know, to recognize)

Present		Preterite	
conozco	conocemos	conocí	conocimos
conoces	conocéis	conociste	conocisteis
conoce	conocen	conoció	conocieron

Imperfect		Present Subjunctive	
conocía	conocíamos	conozca	conozcamos
conocías	conocíais	conozcas	conozcáis
conocía	conocían	conozca	conozcan

contar (to count, to tell)

Present		Preterite	
cuento	contamos	conté	contamos
cuentas	contáis	contaste	contasteis
cuenta	cuentan	contó	contaron

Imperfect		Present Subjunctive	
contaba	contábamos	cuente	contemos
contabas	contabais	cuentes	contéis
contaba	contaban	cuente	cuenten

continuar (to continue)

Present		Preterite	
continúo	continuamos	continué	continuamos
continúas	continuáis	continuaste	continuasteis
continúa	continúan	continuó	continuaron

Imperfect		Present Subjunctive	
continuaba	continuábamos	continúe	continuemos
continuabas	continuabais	continúes	continuéis
continuaba	continuaban	continúe	continúen

correr (to run)

Present		Preterite	
corro	corremos	corrí	corrimos
corres	corréis	corriste	corristeis
corre	corren	corrió	corrieron

Imperfect		Present Subjunctive	
corría	corríamos	corra	corramos
corrías	corríais	corras	corráis
corría	corrían	corra	corran

costar (to cost)

Present		Preterite	
—	—		
—	—		
cuesta	cuestan	costó	costaron

Imperfect		Present Subjunctive	
—	—		
—	—		
costaba	costaban	cueste	cuesten

D

dar (to give)

Present		Preterite	
doy	damos	di	dimos
das	dais	diste	disteis
da	dan	dio	dieron

Imperfect		Present Subjunctive	
daba	dábamos	dé	demos
dabas	dabais	des	deis
daba	daban	dé	den

decir (to say, to tell)

Present		Preterite	
digo	decimos	dije	dijimos
dices	decís	dijiste	dijisteis
dice	dicen	dijo	dijeron

Imperfect		Present Subjunctive	
decía	decíamos	diga	digamos
decías	decíais	digas	digáis
decía	decían	diga	digan

defender (to defend)

Present		Preterite	
defiendo	defendemos	defendí	defendimos
defiendes	defendéis	defendiste	defendisteis
defiende	defienden	defendió	defendieron

Imperfect		Present Subjunctive	
defendía	defendíamos	defienda	defendamos
defendías	defendíais	defiendas	defendáis
defendía	defendían	defienda	defiendan

despertar (to wake)

Present		Preterite	
despierto	despertamos	desperté	despertamos
despiertas	despertáis	despertaste	despertasteis
despierta	despiertan	despertó	despertaron

Imperfect		Present Subjunctive	
despertaba	despertábamos	despierte	despertemos
despertabas	despertabais	despiertes	despertéis
despertaba	despertaban	despierte	despierten

destruir (to destroy)

Present		Preterite	
destruyo	destruimos	destruí	destruimos
destruyes	destruís	destruiste	destruisteis
destruye	destruyen	destruyó	destruyeron

Imperfect		Present Subjunctive	
destruía	destruíamos	destruya	destruyamos
destruías	destruíais	destruyas	destruyáis
destruía	destruían	destruya	destruyan

devolver (to return)

Present		Preterite	
devuelvo	devolvemos	devolví	devolvimos
devuelves	devolvéis	devolviste	devolvisteis
devuelve	devuelven	devolvió	devolvieron

Imperfect		Present Subjunctive	
devolvía	devolvíamos	devuelva	devolvamos
devolvías	devolvíais	devuelvas	devolváis
devolvía	devolvían	devuelva	devuelvan

distribuir (to distribute)

Present		Preterite	
distribuyo	distribuimos	distribuí	distribuimos
distribuyes	distribuís	distribuiste	distribuisteis
distribuye	distribuyen	distribuyó	distribuyeron

Imperfect		Present Subjunctive	
distribuía	distribuíamos	distribuya	distribuyamos
distribuías	distribuíais	distribuyas	distribuyáis
distribuía	distribuían	distribuya	distribuyan

dormir (to sleep)

Present		Preterite	
duermo	dormimos	dormí	dormimos
duermes	dormís	dormiste	dormisteis
duerme	duermen	durmió	durmieron

Imperfect		Present Subjuncctive	
dormía	dormíamos	duerma	durmamos
dormías	dormíais	duermas	durmáis
dormía	dormían	duerma	duerman

E

empezar   (to start, to begin)

Present		Preterite	
empiezo	empezamos	empecé	empezamos
empiezas	empezáis	empezaste	empezasteis
empieza	empiezan	empezó	empezaron

Imperfect		Present Subjunctive	
empezaba	empezábamos	empiece	empecemos
empezabas	empezabais	empieces	empecéis
empezaba	empezaban	empiece	empiecen

entender   (to understand)

Present		Preterite	
entiendo	entendemos	entendí	entendimos
entiendes	entendéis	entendiste	entendisteis
entiende	entienden	entendió	entendieron

Imperfect		Present Subjunctive	
entendía	entendíamos	entienda	entendamos
entendías	entendíais	entiendas	entendáis
entendía	entendían	entienda	entiendan

enviar   (to send)

Present		Preterite	
envío	enviamos	envié	enviamos
envías	enviáis	enviaste	enviasteis
envía	envían	envió	enviaron

Imperfect		Present Subjunctive	
enviaba	enviábamos	envíe	enviemos
enviabas	enviabais	envíes	enviéis
enviaba	enviaban	envíe	envíen

escribir (to write)

Present		Preterite	
escribo	escribimos	escribí	escribimos
escribes	escribís	escribiste	escribisteis
escribe	escriben	escribió	escribieron

Imperfect		Present Subjunctive	
escribía	escribíamos	escriba	escribamos
escribías	escribíais	escribas	escribáis
escribía	escribían	escriba	escriban

estar (to be)

Present		Preterite	
estoy	estamos	estuve	estuvimos
estás	estáis	estuviste	estuvisteis
está	están	estuvo	estuvieron

Imperfect		Present Subjunctive	
estaba	estábamos	esté	estemos
estabas	estabais	estés	estéis
estaba	estaban	esté	estén

estudiar (to study)

Present		Preterite	
estudio	estudiamos	estudié	estudiamos
estudias	estudiáis	estudiaste	estudiasteis
estudia	estudian	estudió	estudiaron

Imperfect		Present Subjunctive	
estudiaba	estudiábamos	estudie	estudiemos
estudiabas	estudiabais	estudies	estudiéis
estudiaba	estudiaban	estudie	estudien

G

guiar (to guide, to lead)			
Present		**Preterite**	
guío	guiamos	guié	guiamos
guías	guiáis	guiaste	guiasteis
guía	guían	guió	guiaron
Imperfect		**Present Subjunctive**	
guiaba	guiábamos	guíe	guiemos
guiabas	guiabais	guíes	guiéis
guiaba	guiaban	guíe	guíen

H

haber (to have)			
Present		**Preterite**	
he	hemos	hube	hubimos
has	habéis	hubiste	hubisteis
ha	han	hubo	hubieron
Imperfect		**Present Subjunctive**	
había	habíamos	haya	hayamos
habías	habíais	hayas	hayáis
había	habían	haya	hayan

hacer (to do, to make)			
Present		**Preterite**	
hago	hacemos	hice	hicimos
haces	hacéis	hiciste	hicisteis
hace	hacen	hizo	hicieron
Imperfect		**Present Subjunctive**	
hacía	hacíamos	haga	hagamos
hacías	hacíais	hagas	hagáis
hacía	hacían	haga	hagan

I

incluir (to include)			
Present		**Preterite**	
incluyo	incluimos	incluí	incluimos
incluyes	incluís	incluiste	incluisteis
incluye	incluyen	incluyó	incluyeron
Imperfect		**Present Subjunctive**	
incluía	incluíamos	incluya	incluyamos
incluías	incluíais	incluyas	incluyáis
incluía	incluían	incluya	incluyan

ir (to go)			
Present		**Preterite**	
voy	vamos	fui	fuimos
vas	vais	fuiste	fuisteis
va	van	fue	fueron
Imperfect		**Present Subjunctive**	
iba	íbamos	vaya	vayamos
ibas	ibais	vayas	vayáis
iba	iban	vaya	vayan

J

jugar (to play)			
Present		**Preterite**	
juego	jugamos	jugué	jugamos
juegas	jugáis	jugaste	jugasteis
juega	juegan	jugó	jugaron
Imperfect		**Present Subjunctive**	
jugaba	jugábamos	juegue	juguemos
jugabas	jugabais	juegues	juguéis
jugaba	jugaban	juegue	jueguen

L

leer (to read)

Present		Preterite	
leo	leemos	leí	leímos
lees	leéis	leíste	leísteis
lee	leen	leyó	leyeron

Imperfect		Present Subjunctive	
leía	leíamos	lea	leamos
leías	leíais	leas	leáis
leía	leían	lea	lean

llegar (to arrive)

Present		Preterite	
llego	llegamos	llegué	llegamos
llegas	llegáis	llegaste	llegasteis
llega	llegan	llegó	llegan

Imperfect		Present Subjunctive	
llegaba	llegábamos	llegue	lleguemos
llegabas	llegabais	llegues	lleguéis
llegaba	llegaban	llegue	lleguen

llevar (to take)

Present		Preterite	
llevo	llevamos	llevé	llevamos
llevas	lleváis	llevaste	llevasteis
lleva	llevan	llevó	llevaron

Imperfect		Present Subjunctive	
llevaba	llevábamos	lleve	llevemos
llevabas	llevabais	lleves	llevéis
llevaba	llevaban	lleve	lleven

M

mentir (to lie)

Present		Preterite	
miento	mentimos	mentí	mentimos
mientes	mentís	mentíste	mentisteis
miente	mienten	mintió	mintieron
Imperfect		**Present Subjunctive**	
mentía	mentíamos	mienta	mentamos
mentías	mentíais	mientas	mentáis
mentía	mentían	mienta	mientan

mover (to move)

Present		Preterite	
muevo	movemos	moví	movimos
mueves	movéis	moviste	movisteis
mueve	mueven	movió	movieron
Imperfect		**Present Subjunctive**	
movía	movíamos	mueva	movamos
movías	movíais	muevas	mováis
movía	movían	mueva	muevan

O

oír (to hear)

Present		Preterite	
oigo	oímos	oí	oímos
oyes	oís	oíste	oísteis
oye	oyen	oyó	oyeron
Imperfect		**Present Subjunctive**	
oía	oíamos	oiga	oigamos
oías	oíais	oigas	oigáis
oía	oían	oiga	oigan

P

parecer (to appear, to resemble)

Present		Preterite	
parezco	parecemos	parecí	parecimos
pareces	parecéis	pareciste	parecisteis
parece	parecen	pareció	parecieron

Imperfect		Present Subjunctive	
parecía	parecíamos	parezca	parezcamos
parecías	parecíais	parezcas	parezcáis
parecía	parecían	parezca	parezcan

pedir (to ask for, to request)

Present		Preterite	
pido	pedimos	pedí	pedimos
pides	pedís	pediste	pedisteis
pide	piden	pidió	pidieron

Imperfect		Present Subjunctive	
pedía	pedíamos	pida	pidamos
pedías	pedíais	pidas	pidáis
pedía	pedían	pida	pidan

pensar (to think)

Present		Preterite	
pienso	pensamos	pensé	pensamos
piensas	pensáis	pensaste	pensasteis
piensa	piensan	pensó	pensaron

Imperfect		Present Subjunctive	
pensaba	pensábamos	piense	pensemos
pensabas	pensabais	pienses	penséis
pensaba	pensaban	piense	piensen

perder (to lose)

Present		Preterite	
pierdo	perdemos	perdí	perdimos
pierdes	perdéis	perdiste	perdisteis
pierde	pierden	perdió	perdieron

Imperfect		Present Subjunctive	
perdía	perdíamos	pierda	perdamos
perdías	perdíais	pierdas	perdáis
perdía	perdían	pierda	pierdan

poder (to be able to)

Present		Preterite	
puedo	podemos	pude	pudimos
puedes	podéis	pudiste	pudisteis
puede	pueden	pudo	pudieron

Imperfect		Present Subjunctive	
podía	podíamos	pueda	podamos
podías	podíais	puedas	podáis
podía	podían	pueda	puedan

poner (to put)

Present		Preterite	
pongo	ponemos	puse	pusimos
pones	ponéis	pusiste	pusisteis
pone	ponen	puso	pusieron

Imperfect		Present Subjunctive	
ponía	poníamos	ponga	pongamos
ponías	poníais	pongas	pongáis
ponía	ponían	ponga	pongan

preferir (to prefer)

Present		Preterite	
prefiero	preferimos	preferí	preferimos
prefieres	preferís	preferiste	preferisteis
prefiere	prefieren	prefirió	prefirieron

Imperfect		Present Subjunctive	
prefería	preferíamos	prefiera	preferamos
preferías	preferíais	prefieras	preferáis
prefería	preferían	prefiera	prefieran

preparar (to prepare)

Present		Preterite	
preparo	preparamos	preparé	preparamos
preparas	preparáis	preparaste	preparasteis
prepara	preparan	preparó	prepararon
Imperfect		**Present Subjunctive**	
preparaba	preparábamos	prepare	preparemos
preparabas	preparabais	prepares	preparéis
preparaba	preparaban	prepare	preparen

producir (to produce)

Present		Preterite	
produzco	producimos	produje	produjimos
produces	producís	produjiste	produjisteis
produce	producen	produjo	produjeron
Imperfect		**Present Subjunctive**	
producía	producíamos	produzca	produzcamos
producías	producíais	produzcas	produzcáis
producía	producían	produzca	produzcan

Q

querer (to want)

Present		Preterite	
quiero	queremos	quise	quisimos
quieres	queréis	quisiste	quisisteis
quiere	quieren	quiso	quisieron
Imperfect		**Present Subjunctive**	
quería	queríamos	quiera	queramos
querías	queríais	quieras	queráis
quería	querían	quiera	quieran

R

recordar (to remember)

Present		Preterite	
recuerdo	recordamos	recordé	recordamos
recuerdas	recordáis	recordaste	recordasteis
recuerda	recuerdan	recordó	recordaron

Imperfect		Present Subjunctive	
recordaba	recordábamos	recuerde	recordemos
recordabas	recordabais	recuerdes	recordéis
recordaba	recordaban	recuerde	recuerden

regresar (to return, to come back)

Present		Preterite	
regreso	regresamos	regresé	regresamos
regresas	regresáis	regresaste	regresasteis
regresa	regresan	regresó	regresaron

Imperfect		Present Subjunctive	
regresaba	regresábamos	regrese	regresemos
regresabas	regresabais	regreses	regreséis
regresaba	regresaban	regrese	regresen

repetir (to repeat)

Present		Preterite	
repito	repetimos	repetí	repetimos
repites	repetís	repetiste	repetisteis
repite	repiten	repitió	repitieron

Imperfect		Present Subjunctive	
repetía	repetíamos	repita	repitamos
repetías	repetíais	repitas	repitáis
repetía	repetían	repita	repitan

S

saber (to know)

Present		Preterite	
sé	sabemos	supe	supimos
sabes	sabéis	supiste	supisteis
sabe	saben	supo	supieron
Imperfect		**Present Subjunctive**	
sabía	sabíamos	sepa	sepamos
sabías	sabíais	sepas	sepáis
sabía	sabían	sepa	sepan

sacar (to take out)

Present		Preterite	
saco	sacamos	saqué	sacamos
sacas	sacáis	sacaste	sacasteis
saca	sacan	sacó	sacaron
Imperfect		**Present Subjunctive**	
sacaba	sacábamos	saque	saquemos
sacabas	sacabais	saques	saquéis
sacaba	sacaban	saque	saquen

salir (to go out, to exit)

Present		Preterite	
salgo	salimos	salí	salimos
sales	salís	saliste	salisteis
sale	salen	salió	salieron
Imperfect		**Present Subjunctive**	
salía	salíamos	salga	salgamos
salías	salíais	salgas	salgáis
salía	salían	salga	salgan

saludar (to greet)

Present		Preterite	
saludo	saludamos	saludé	saludamos
saludas	saludáis	saludaste	saludasteis
saluda	saludan	saludó	saludaron
Imperfect		**Present Subjunctive**	
saludaba	saludábamos	salude	saludemos
saludabas	saludabais	saludes	saludéis
saludaba	saludaban	salude	saluden

sentir (to feel)

Present		Preterite	
siento	sentimos	sentí	sentimos
sientes	sentís	sentiste	sentisteis
siente	sienten	sintió	sintieron
Imperfect		**Present Subjunctive**	
sentía	sentíamos	sienta	sintamos
sentías	sentíais	sientas	sintáis
sentía	sentían	sienta	sientan

ser (to be)

Present		Preterite	
soy	somos	fui	fuimos
eres	sois	fuiste	fuisteis
es	son	fue	fueron
Imperfect		**Present Subjunctive**	
era	éramos	sea	seamos
eras	erais	seas	seáis
era	eran	sea	sean

servir (to serve)

Present		Preterite	
sirvo	servimos	serví	servimos
sirves	servís	serviste	servisteis
sirve	sirven	sirvió	sirvieron
Imperfect		**Present Subjunctive**	
servía	servíamos	sirva	sirvamos
servías	servíais	sirvas	sirváis
servía	servían	sirva	sirvan

suponer (to suppose)

Present		Preterite	
supongo	suponemos	supuse	supusimos
supones	suponéis	supusiste	supusisteis
supone	suponen	supuso	supusieron

Imperfect		Present Subjunctive	
suponía	suponíamos	suponga	supongamos
suponías	suponíais	supongas	supongáis
suponía	suponían	suponga	supongan

T

tener (to have)

Present		Preterite	
tengo	tenemos	tuve	tuvimos
tienes	tenéis	tuviste	tuvisteis
tiene	tienen	tuvo	tuvieron

Imperfect		Present Subjunctive	
tenía	teníamos	tenga	tengamos
tenías	teníais	tengas	tengáis
tenía	tenían	tenga	tengan

tomar (to take, drink)

Present		Preterite	
tomo	tomamos	tomé	tomamos
tomas	tomáis	tomaste	tomasteis
toma	toman	tomó	tomaron

Imperfect		Present Subjunctive	
tomaba	tomábamos	tome	tomemos
tomabas	tomabais	tomes	toméis
tomaba	tomaban	tome	tomen

traer   (to bring)

Present		Preterite	
traigo	traemos	traje	trajimos
traes	traéis	trajiste	trajisteis
trae	traen	trajo	trajeron
Imperfect		**Present Subjunctive**	
traía	traíamos	traiga	traigamos
traías	traíais	traigas	traigáis
traía	traían	traiga	traigan

V

venir   (to come)

Present		Preterite	
vengo	venimos	vine	vinimos
vienes	venís	viniste	vinisteis
viene	vienen	vino	vinieron
Imperfect		**Present Subjunctive**	
venía	veníamos	venga	vengamos
venías	veníais	vengas	vengáis
venía	venían	venga	vengan

ver   (to see)

Present		Preterite	
veo	vemos	vi	vimos
ves	veis	viste	visteis
ve	ven	vio	vieron
Imperfect		**Present Subjunctive**	
veía	veíamos	vea	veamos
veías	veíais	veas	veáis
veía	veían	vea	vean

vestir (to dress)

Present		Preterite	
visto	vestimos	vestí	vestimos
vistes	vestís	vestíste	vestisteis
viste	visten	vistió	vistieron

Imperfect		Present Subjunctive	
vestía	vestíamos	vista	vistamos
vestías	vestíais	vistas	vistáis
vestía	vestían	vista	vistan

vivir (to live)

Present		Preterite	
vivo	vivimos	viví	vivimos
vives	vivís	viviste	vivisteis
vive	viven	vivió	vivieron

Imperfect		Present Subjunctive	
vivía	vivíamos	viva	vivamos
vivías	vivíais	vivas	viváis
vivía	vivían	viva	vivan

volver (to return, to come back)

Present		Preterite	
vuelvo	volvemos	volví	volvimos
vuelves	volvéis	volviste	volvisteis
vuelve	vuelven	volvió	volvieron

Imperfect		Present Subjunctive	
volvía	volvíamos	vuelva	volvamos
volvías	volvíais	vuelvas	volváis
volvía	volvían	vuelva	vuelvan

Appendix C
Accent Marks

Written Accent Marks

There is more to learning Spanish than just memorizing verb forms and other such constructions. You also need to know how to use written accent marks. Here is the terminology and the five rules you need to know.

TERMINOLOGY

First of all, you need to learn the right terminology: *grave* (or *llana*), *aguda*, and *esdrújula*.

A *palabra* (word) *llana* (or *grave*) has the stress on the second-to-last syllable: **mesa** *(MEH-sah)*. A *palabra aguda* has the stress on the last syllable: **salón** *(sah-LOHN)*. A *palabra esdrújula* has the stress on any syllable that comes before the second-to-last syllable: **pájaro** *(PAH-jah-roh)*.

Next we'll teach you more about these three types of words, as well as how to determine which of them carry accent marks.

RULE #1, PALABRAS AGUDAS

A *palabra aguda* is a word that is stressed on its final syllable. For example:

> volcán   *(vol-CAHN)*   volcano
> papel   *(pah-PEHL)*   paper
> mamá   *(mah-MAH)*   mom

> **Rule #1** *If a word is a palabra aguda AND it ends in -n, -s, or a vowel, place an accent mark on the final vowel.*

Rule #1 is illustrated by some of the words you learned in Lesson 2.

▶ This word is a *palabra aguda*, but it ends in *-d*. No accent mark.

libert**ad**   *(lee-behr-TAHD)*

▶ This word is a *palabra aguda*, and it ends in *-n*. Add an accent mark.

condici**ón**   *(cohn-dee-SEEOHN)*

▶ This word is a *palabra aguda*, and it ends in a vowel. Add an accent mark.

pap**á**   *(pah-PAH)*

RULE #2, PALABRAS LLANAS (GRAVES)

A *palabra llana* (also called *grave*) is a word that is stressed on its second-to-last syllable. For example:

belleza   *(beh-YEH-sah)*   beauty
álbum   *(AHL-boom)*   album
madre   *(MAH-dreh)*   madre

> **Rule #2** If a word is a palabra llana *and it* **DOESN'T** *end in* -n, -s, *or a vowel, place an accent mark on the second-to-last vowel.*

Rule #2 is illustrated by some of the words you learned in Lesson 3.

▶ This word is a *palabra llana*, and it ends in *-l*. Add an accent mark.

fá**cil**   *(FAH-seel)*

▶ This word is a *palabra llana*, but it ends with a vowel. No accent mark.

roj**a**   *(ROH-hah)*

RULE #3, PALABRAS ESDRÚJULAS

A *palabra esdrújula* has the stress on any syllable that comes before the second-to-last syllable.

> pájaro   *(PAH-jah-roh)*   *bird*
> matemática   *(mah-teh-MAH-tee-cah)*   *math*

> **Rule #3** *If a word is a* palabra esdrújula, *it automatically carries an accent on the stressed vowel.*

▸ The word *esdrújula* is a *palabra esdrújula*, and therefore carries an accent on the *u*.

RULE #4, HOMONYMS

In Spanish, there is a special accent mark used to distinguish between two homonyms, or words that have the same spellings but different meanings. Look at the following examples:

el	article: *the*	él	subject pronoun: *he*
tu	possessive adjective: *your*	tú	subject pronoun: *you*
si	conjunction: *if*	sí	interjection: *yes*
mi	possessive adjective: *my*	mí	object pronoun: *me*

> **Rule #4** *Generally, one of two homonyms will carry an accent on the vowel of the stressed syllable.*

RULE #5, REFLEXIVE VERBS AND THE PRESENT PROGRESSIVE

Take a look at what happens with a reflexive verb is used in the present progressive.

peinar   →   peinando   →   Estoy peinándome el pelo. *(pey-NAHN-doh-seh)*   *I am combing my hair.*

bañar   →   bañando   →   Estoy bañándome. *(bah-nyAHn-doh-seh)* *I am bathing [myself].*

Rule #5 *When a reflexive verb is used in the present progressive, an accent mark is added to keep the original stress.*

Appendix D
Answer Key

Lesson 1

PART 1, Exercise A

1. h
2. c
3. g
4. i
5. a
6. d
7. b
8. e
9. j
10. f

Exercise B

1. b
2. b
3. c
4. a
5. c

PART 2, Exercise A

1. sensación
2. depresión
3. pesimismo
4. invención
5. celebración
6. curioso
7. urgente
8. prosperidad
9. experiencia
10. optimismo

Exercise B

1. geography
2. artist
3. pharmacy
4. nation
5. fabulous
6. paradise
7. humanity
8. dormitory
9. professor
10. museum

PART 3, Exercise A

1. Hola
2. Hasta luego
3. Me llamo
4. Cómo te llamas
5. Buenos días

Lesson 2

PART 1, Exercise A

1. la
2. la
3. la
4. el
5. el
6. la
7. el
8. el
9. la
10. el/la

Exercise B

1. unas nueces
2. un águila
3. unos mapas
4. una pluma
5. unas fotos

Exercise C

1. el garaje
2. la decisión
3. los relojes
4. el barril
5. las motos

PART 2, Exercise A

1. d
2. h
3. i
4. f
5. b
6. a
7. e
8. g
9. c
10. j

Exercise B

1. Son las tres y quince/cuarto de la tarde.
2. Es la una y diez de la mañana.
3. Son las cuatro y cincuenta de la tarde. / Son las cinco menos diez de la tarde.
4. Son las ocho y quince/cuarto de la tarde.
5. Son las nueve de la mañana.
6. Son las tres y quince/cuarto de la tarde.
7. Son las dos de la tarde.
8. Son las once de la mañana.
9. Es mediodía. / Son las doce de la tarde.
10. Es medianoche. / Son las doce de la mañana.

Lesson 3

PART 1, Exercise A

1. saludar

Person	Singular	Plural
1st	yo saludo	nosotros saludamos nosotras saludamos
2nd	tú saludas	vosotros saludáis vosotras saludáis
3rd	él saluda ella saluda usted saluda	ellos saludan ellas saludan ustedes saludan

2. aprender

Person	Singular	Plural
1st	yo aprendo	nosotros aprendemos nosotras aprendemos
2nd	tú aprendes	vosotros aprendéis vosotras aprendéis
3rd	él aprende ella aprende usted aprende	ellos aprenden ellas aprenden ustedes aprenden

Exercise B

1. corre
2. viven
3. abro
4. estudiáis
5. comes
6. preparamos
7. lee
8. escriben
9. comprendo
10. regresáis

Exercise C

1. Correct
2. Tú preparas la tarea.
3. Correct
4. Vosotros vivéis en los Estados Unidos.
5. Miguel estudia el inglés.

PART 2, Exercise A

1. sesenta y cinco dólares
2. treinta y un lápices
3. cien libros
4. ochenta y dos flores
5. cincuenta mochilas

Exercise B

1. ¿Estudia Jorge en la universidad?
2. ¿Canta ella?
3. ¿Son buenos los profesores?
4. ¿Tiene 19 años Iris?
5. ¿Eres [tú] de Guatemala?

Exercise C

1. cuántos
2. dónde
3. quién
4. cuánta
5. cuándo

Lesson 4

PART 1, Exercise A

1. guapas
2. joven
3. buenos
4. vieja
5. feliz

Exercise B

1. a
2. a
3. b
4. b
5. a

Exercise C

1. Tengo un carro nuevo. / Tengo un nuevo carro.
2. Ese perro es grande. / Es grande ese perro.
3. Es hermosa Emilia. / Emilia es hermosa.
4. Vuestras mochilas son esas. / Esas mochilas son vuestras.
5. ¿Es tuyo aquel libro? / ¿Aquel libro es tuyo?

PART 2, Exercise A

1. soy
2. está
3. es
4. está
5. es

Exercise B

1. b
2. b
3. a
4. b
5. b

Exercise C

1. mil cien niñas
2. dos millones quinientos veinte insectos
3. dos mil libros
4. seiscientos escuelas
5. mil trescientos diez señores

Lesson 5

PART 1, Exercise A

1. b
2. c
3. a
4. d
5. e
6. f

Exercise B

1. pensar

Person	Singular	Plural
1st	yo pienso	nosotros pensamos
		nosotras pensamos
2nd	tú piensas	vosotros pensáis
		vosotras pensáis
3rd	él piensa	ellos piensan
	ella piensa	ellas piensan
	usted piensa	ustedes piensan

2. destruir

Person	Singular	Plural
1st	yo destruyo	nosotros destruimos
		nosotras destruimos
2nd	tú destruyes	vosotros destruís
		vosotras destruís
3rd	él destruye	ellos destruyen
	ella destruye	ellas destruyen
	usted destruye	ustedes destruyen

PART 2, Exercise A

1. doy
2. eres
3. vais
4. conozco
5. tiene

Exercise B

1. a
2. c
3. a
4. b
5. c

Exercise C

1. Los señores están leyendo el periódico.
2. El bebé esta durmiendo.
3. Mi madre me está pidiendo un café.
4. Yo estoy escribiendo una carta postal a mi amiga.
5. Ellos le están dando una cobija.
6. Nosotros estamos comiendo la cena.
7. Raúl y Juliana están estudiando para el examen.
8. La niña está llorando.
9. La profesora está hablando.
10. Mi abuela está cocinando.

Lesson 6

PART 1, Exercise A

1. Soy
2. Es
3. Estáis
4. Eres
5. Son
6. es
7. Somos
8. Están
9. es
10. Estás

Exercise B

1. Mi jefe es rico.
2. Francisca tiene nuevo años.
3. Tomamos leche.
4. Los niños saben hablar alemán.
5. Hay dos manzanas en la refrigeradora.
6. ¿Tomas el autobús a la escuela?

PART 2, Exercise A

1. Francisco lo tiene.
2. ¿Lo veis?
3. La leemos.
4. El muchacho lo escribe.
5. Yo la veo.

Exercise B

1. les
2. nos
3. me
4. le
5. le

Exercise C

1. Te los mando.
2. Se la presto.
3. Se la enseño.
4. Nos la compra.
5. ¿Me la traes?

Exercise D

1. vamos al
2. voy al
3. vais a la
4. van a la
5. van al

Lesson 7

PART 1, Exercise A

1. Ninguno de mis amigos vive ahí.
2. No necesitamos nada.
3. Nunca estudio con nadie.
4. ¿No queréis ir a la fiesta?
5. No hay nada en la refrigeradora.
6. Nunca coméis desayuno.
7. No conozco a ningún niño americano.
8. Nunca voy al gimnasio.
9. Los alumnos no tienen una computadora.
10. No amo a nadie.

Exercise B

1. tampoco
2. sino
3. también
4. pero
5. también
6. sino
7. pero
8. tampoco
9. también
10. sino

PART 2, Exercise A

1. vendió
2. comí
3. corristeis
4. cerraste
5. llegó
6. ganó
7. escribisteis
8. estudió
9. vivió
10. comprendí

Exercise B

1. compartí
2. comimos
3. vivisteis
4. compraste
5. vendieron
6. escribió
7. celebré
8. preparó
9. recibí
10. enseñó

Exercise C

1. me gusta
2. le gusta
3. nos gusta
4. les gusta
5. le gustan
6. os gustan
7. te gusta
8. le gusta
9. les gusta
10. nos gusta

Lesson 8

PART 1, Exercise A

1. durmió
2. prefirió
3. llegamos
4. dio
5. dije

Exercise B

1. Conocimos al nuevo profesor ayer.
2. Anoche pude terminar mi tarea.
3. Nancy finalmente supo la verdad.
4. Quisieron comprar un carro nuevo, pero no tenían suficiente dinero.

PART 2, Exercise A

1. Me baño todos los días.
2. Zoila se prueba los zapatos.
3. Mi padre se alza a las 6 de la mañana.
4. La señora se quita los lentes.
5. ¿Te lavas la cara en la mañana?
6. Mi mejor amigo se enoja.
7. Federico se duerme a las 11.
8. La profesora se sienta sobre el escritorio.

Exercise B

1. cansarse

Person	Singular	Plural
1st	yo me canso	nosotros nos cansamos
		nosotras nos cansamos
2nd	tú te cansas	vosotros os cansáis
		vosotras os cansáis
3rd	él se cansa	ellos se cansan
	ella se cansa	ellas se cansan
	usted se cansa	ustedes se cansan

2. enojarse

Person	Singular	Plural
1st	yo me enojo	nosotros nos enojamos
		nosotras nos enojamos
2nd	tú te enojas	vosotros os enojáis
		vosotras os enojáis
3rd	él se enoja	ellos se enojan
	ella se enoja	ellas se enojan
	usted se enoja	ustedes se enojan

3. irse

Person	Singular	Plural
1st	yo me voy	nosotros nos vamos
		nosotras nos vamos
2nd	tú te vas	vosotros os vais
		vosotras os vais
3rd	él se va	ellos se van
	ella se va	ellas se van
	usted se va	ustedes se van

4. reírse

Person	Singular	Plural
1st	yo me río	nosotros nos reímos
		nosotras nos reímos
2nd	tú te ríes	vosotros os reís
		vosotras os reís
3rd	él se ríe	ellos se ríen
	ella se ríe	ellas se ríen
	usted se ríe	ustedes se ríen

Lesson 9

PART 1, Exercise A

1. más
2. menos
3. tanto como
4. más
5. mejor
6. tanta
7. menos
8. menor
9. peor
10. más

Exercise B

1. el niño más paciente
2. la señora menos diplomática
3. la chica menos inteligente
4. el libro mejor
5. la abuela menos vieja
6. el hombre peor
7. el ejercicio más facil
. el carro menos rápido
. la casa más pequeña
10. la camisa menos cara

Exercise C

1. El pan es riquísimo.
2. La niña es traviesísima.
3. El profesor es malísimo.
4. La calle es larguísima.
5. Estoy felicísimo/a.

PART 2, Exercise A

1. El gato está debajo de la mesa.
2. El gato está dentro de la caja.
3. El gato está encima de la cama.
4. El gato está delante de la televisión.
5. El gato está lejos de la niña.

Exercise B

1. b
2. b
3. a
4. c
5. c
6. b
7. a
8. c

PART 3, Exercise A

1. cuál
2. cuál
3. cuáles
4. qué
5. cuál

Exercise B

1. ¿Cuál es tu canción favorita?
2. ¿Cuál broma es más chistosa?
3. ¿Cuál camisa te gusta?
4. ¿Cuál quieres?
5. ¿Qué es eso?

Lesson 10

PART 1, Exercise A

1. ibais
2. recibías
3. era
4. leían
5. veíais
6. corrían
7. iban
8. erais
9. tenías
10. llegábamos

Exercise B

1. veía
2. eran
3. aburría
4. esperaba
5. éramos
6. era
7. leías

8. mandabas
9. bañaban
10. vivía, iba

PART 2, Exercise A

1. a
2. b
3. a
4. b
5. a
6. b

Exercise B

1. se levantó
2. era/creía
3. dio
4. empezó
5. lloraba
6. entré/vi
7. era
8. comió
9. olvidó
10. hacía

Exercise C

1. Estábamos comiendo en la cocina. / Comíamos en la cocina.
2. Los estudiantes estaban estudiando español. / Los estudiantes estudiaban español.
3. Mi madre estaba cocinando. / Mi madre cocinaba.
4. Tú estabas viajando en América del Sur. / Tú viajabas en América del Sur.
5. Ustedes estaban escuchando la radio. / Ustedes escuchaban la radio.

Lesson 11

PART 1, Exercise A

1. finalmente
2. nerviosamente
3. claramente
4. raramente
5. brevemente

Exercise B

1. algo
2. muy
3. por supuesto
4. un poco
5. acá
6. luego
7. tanto
8. también
9. siempre
10. mucho

PART 2, Exercise A

1. se buscan
2. se dice
3. se trabaja
4. se descansa
5. se come
6. se juega
7. se duerme
8. se discute
9. se vende
10. se hable

Exercise B

1. b
2. a
3. b
4. a
5. a
6. b

Exercise C

1. estudie
2. coman
3. oigamos
4. duermas
5. ganen
6. vengáis
7. haya
8. seamos
9. veas
10. estéis

Exercise D

1. Hace diez días que estoy en Buenos Aires.
2. ¿Cuánto tiempo hace que su tío vive aquí? / ¿Hace cuánto tiempo que su tío vive aquí?
3. Hace seis meses que nos casamos.
4. Fueron a Quito hace tres años.
5. Hace un día que regresó a los Estados Unidos.

Index

INDEX